# Texas Bad Girls

# TEXAS BAD GIRLS

## Hussies, Harlots, and Horse Thieves

J. Lee Butts

LONE STAR BOOKS

Guilford, Connecticut

## LONE STAR BOOKS

Published by Lone Star Books
An imprint of Globe Pequot
4501 Forbes Boulevard, Suite 200 Lanham, MD 20706

Distributed by NATIONAL BOOK NETWORK

Originally published by Republic of Texas Press

British Library Cataloguing-in-Publication Information available

Library of Congress Cataloging-in-Publication Data available

ISBN 978-1-4930-2616-6 (paperback)
ISBN 978-1-4930-2617-3 (e-book)

♾™ The paper used in this publication meets the minimum requirements of American National Standard for Information Sciences—Permanence of Paper for Printed Library Materials, ANSI/NISO Z39.48-1992.

For my wife Carol, who has always believed in me.

# CONTENTS

———●●———

CONTENTS

# PREFACE

---•••---

Americans love an outlaw. From the very earliest recorded incidences of civil disobedience to the televised trials of modern murderers, we have followed the lives and careers of our darker-natured cousins with what borders on a pathological interest. The American West of myth and legend teemed with such people. Names like Billy the Kid, Jesse James, Butch Cassidy, Clay Allison, and John Wesley Hardin still have the power to sell books and matinee movie tickets. Pat Garrett, Wild Bill Hickok, Bat Masterson, and Wyatt Earp became equally famous for their efforts at trying to make such men "toe the line."

Closely following the plainsmen, cowboys, railroaders, rivermen, settlers, and outlaws, their women tended to blend into the background clutter of children, spirit-breaking work, and early death. But as the old philosopher liked to say, for every rule there are exceptions. The bad girls of the West, and of Texas in particular, tended to be glowing examples of those exceptions. And although Sally Skull, Chipita Rodriguez, and Sarah Bowman have never achieved the name recognition of their more hairy-legged counterparts, Etta Place, Belle Starr, and Bonnie Parker enjoy a degree of fame far exceeding a host of equally gifted male evildoers, gunfighters, and thugs of the last two centuries.

The text that follows is a sometimes humorous, sometimes tongue-in-cheek, sometimes deeply sad and affecting set of biographies of twenty-plus Texas bad girls. We're talking the baddest of the bad, the evilest of the evil, the nastiest of the nasty, and sometimes even the just plain ol' universal royal pain in somebody's aching bazoobus. Husband killers, run-of-the-mill murderers, whorehouse madams, prostitutes, gamblers, bank robbers, floozies, and just everyday hussies, they're all here and each contributes immeasurably to a rowdy, ribald history that dates from the state's earliest settlers to yesterday's biggest news story.

The *bad girls* of Texas prance across the pages of this book in a seamless parade of behavior so far outside the realm of common convention that their places in history were virtually guaranteed even while they lived. The choices they made in lifestyle assured the harshest of societal criticism and condemnation then and now, but our relentless curiosity won't let them rest. Every few years a book like Gail Drago and Ann Ruff's wonderful *Outlaws in Petticoats* appears to remind us that these ladies did exist and that their tumultuous lives contributed greatly to the huge crazy quilt of our shared history. This in spite of the fact that some who deem themselves the keepers of the flame that is our past would prefer that such women simply slide into historic oblivion.

The sheer depth and variety of their unfettered behavior is a thing to behold in and of itself. Sally Skull drove horses and cattle in South Texas, smuggled guns, fought with pistols, and pretty much dared anyone to get in her way. Everyone knew you didn't stop ol' Sally and go through her herds looking for strays because it could get you shot. She married a number of times and is believed to have personally disposed of at least one of her husbands. Chipita Rodriguez made the mistake of being in the wrong place at the wrong time and ended up dangling from the limb of a tree for it. For more than a century it was believed her hanging was the only *legal* execution carried out on a woman in Texas. Fannie Porter, Mary Porter, Tillie Howard, Fat Alice Abbot, Jessie Williams, and Edna Milton worked the management end of the world's oldest profession with all the ups and downs, and ins and outs of such an avocation. Sarah Bowman and Beulah Morose—and perhaps Sophia Porter and Etta Place—all plied the "soiled dove" trade at some point during their lives. Belle Starr and Nance Hill stole horses, drank, gambled, and fought anyone who questioned their behavior in much the same way you would expect of aggressive men over-amped on testosterone. Adah Isaacs Menken and Janis Joplin led astonishingly short, meteoric lives as entertainers and purveyors of their own form of popular culture at the time. The beautiful and mysterious Lottie Deno sat at poker's green felt tables with some of the Old West's most famous and infamous gamblers, gunmen, and grifters. And Karla Faye Tucker, well Karla Faye did it all.

Anyone who reads or studies much has to admit that history is a fickle thing. The forever shifting boundary that divides one man's fact from another's fairy tale often proves hard to pin down. It isn't unusual to find a variety of versions, times, and circumstances for a single incident. When you have someone like Adah Isaacs Menken telling and retelling her own life story for the benefit of gullible writers and reporters who had no way to check the facts, you end up with a mind-boggling level of stupefaction that results in a kind of one from column A, one from column B method of historical reportage. Such is the case with *Texas Bad Girls*. If dates, places, and times don't quite match what you as the reader feel are correct, you have the writer's permission to take a pencil, scratch through that offensive piece of bull feathers, and add whatever butters your biscuits. Unfortunately, prior to the middle of the twentieth century, information about most women of the wild and woolly West is based on myth, legend, sketchy public records, second- to fourth-hand retellings, outright fabrications, and little else. Ladies of questionable background rarely kept diaries or journals and in most instances neither sought nor wanted public attention. As a consequence, dates, name spellings, and hard facts got poorly treated or embellished *most* of the time.

Whether you believe in rugged individualism for men and women alike or that the tough, independent gals in this book were just a bunch of hormone-driven twits who should have stayed at home with the kids, you can't come away from their stories without being completely supportive of their behavior or absolutely appalled by it. Not much middle ground exists for most of them. But in the end what just might matter most may well be the fact of their having been able to live such lives at all. As the benefactors of their passing, we are better off in some instances and much worse off in others. When *Texas Bad Girls* rides across those little gray folds in your brain, you get to judge for yourself—one way or the other.

The author intended these stories to sound to your reader's ear as though a friend just sat down and decided to tell you an interesting tale about someone he once knew. If that philosophical technique worked, this will be an enjoyable experience, and any reader should, above all else, have fun! *Most* of the ladies described on these pages seemed to have had a high old time and can be easily approached with a smile on your face. So saddle up buckaroos and buckarettes, a bevy of Texas's baddest girls are waiting just a turned page away.

# ACKNOWLEDGMENTS

How do you thank all the people who helped in an enterprise such as this? The physical act of writing tends to be done alone and with no overtly noticeable help from anyone—usually in the nude while munching on an endless supply of chocolate chip cookies. At least it seems that way to the uninitiated who typically aren't paying the strictest of attention. Truth is that behind every good writer's incredibly expensive flat-screened liquid crystal CRT lurks an army of little-seen worker bees who toil endlessly for the benefit of the celebrated scribblers whose names get emblazoned on the covers of their thought-provoking masterpieces.

This distinguished tome started as the brainstorm of Steven Jent, RTH (Renowned Texas Historian), me, and a table of buttermilk pancake connoisseurs stranded at Denny's Restaurant in Euless, Texas, one dark and stormy night. Thank you, Charles Shultz. Two cowboys, a vampire, some drunk poets, a red-eyed car salesman, and a waitress shouted encouragement as we loudly abused an acquisitions editor named Ginnie Bivona from the Republic of Texas Press in an effort to get her to cough up a contract and possible up-front money for the project. Did someone say up-front money? Fat chance! The following morning that hardworking and helpful crew down at the Irving Public Library started the literary research ball rolling with an abundance of information and unflagging support that has lasted nigh unto a year. Most of them weren't aware of it, but they did.

As soon as word escaped like a crazed weasel that a publisher had been bamboozled into actually issuing a contract and that said contract had been signed by a somewhat high-strung author, people came out of the woodwork with the names of their favorite Texas bad girls and fabulous arguments as to why those women should be included. A round of special huzzas go to Neil Ross for bringing those feisty Hill gals to my attention. Huzza, huzza, huzza. Neil supplied me with everything I needed for one of my favorite chapters.

As the manuscript progressed, every member of the DFW Writer's Workshop got a chance to take his best evaluator's shot at it during our invaluable read and critique sessions. Large bunches of symbolic roses are hereby thrown to those of you who had only good things to say about my writing skills—you all know who you are. But seriously folks, had it not been for the DFW Writer's Workshop I'd still be living in a refrigerator crate behind the bus station. I owe them my entire writing career to this point.

Extra-special thanks to librarian/archivist Christina Stopka at the Texas Ranger Hall of Fame & Museum in Waco. She treated a mixed-up writer from Dallas like he actually knew what he was doing. If you haven't been to the Hall of Fame, pack granny and the kids and go. Go now. It's less than a block off I-35 and well worth the piddling admission fee.

There's not enough room on this page to express my gratitude to John Anderson with the Archives Division of the Texas State Library. John found a single photograph for me that made my entire trip to Austin and points south worthwhile. In addition he freely guided me to Ester Mes at the Harry Ransom Humanities Research Center. Ester managed to supply me with a photograph of Adah Isaacs Menken I felt certain I'd never find. (She's also extremely good-looking. May have to visit the ol' Harry Ransom again.)

Chris Floerke at the incredible Institute of Texan Cultures made a valiant effort, but couldn't come up with anything quite as low as I needed. I appreciated her friendliness toward and efforts for the strange dude from Dallas who just walked in off the street and started asking to see all the photos in her archive. It has never ceased to amaze me what people will do if you tell them you're a writer.

Most importantly, a thousand heartfelt thanks to Janie Rhodes Burton and her sister Judy, who demonstrated to me beyond any shadow of a doubt that books by unknown authors do get published. And a kiss as delicate as a bluebonnet's petals is blown across Texas to Shreveport where my good friend Roxanne Blackwell Bosserman made me believe what Janie and Judy had shown me with the kind of encouragement money can't buy. She and my brother Mike and his wife Barbara kept cheering when everyone else fell silent.

If I missed anyone, I can't imagine how, so I'll close this out by just repeating two words that sum it all up—Ginnie Bivona. Mil gracias, mi amiga!

# AUTHOR'S NOTE

The author makes no claim to be anything remotely like a serious historian or academician. Any resemblance of the writer of this work to an actual, real, living or dead person of such munificence is purely coincidental and must be regarded with the utmost of suspicion. Should you be one of those folks who just can't stand it unless everything is absolutely accurate and perfect, please consider this as your only warning that the author makes no claim to be either and wouldn't even if he could. If such an attitude just curdles your cream, he suggests you go to the bargain bookrack and buy a two-hundred-year-old classic you've never read, light some candles, open a bottle of wine, fire up a good cigar, and enjoy it all with his blessings.

# CHAPTER 1

——•●•——

# PISTOL PACKIN' MAMA
# Sally Skull

In 1823 an ambitious gristmill operator named William Rabb moved his entire family—children, grandchildren, and all—from Jonesborough, an area now in Red River County, Texas, to a Spanish land grant site in present-day Fayette County, Texas. Tough is the only word that comes to mind when describing such a trip. What people referred to as roads back then lacked a good many of our modern-day conveniences. The muddy, rutted paths amounted to little more than a wide trail into the wilderness. It's a pretty safe bet that Rabb's numerous grandchildren sat in the backs of their fathers' wagons and whined, "Are we there yet?" about ten million times before conclusion of the three-hundred-mile jaunt. The one positive travel note to the whole excursion may have been that "rest areas" were pretty easy to find.

The amazing display of heroism and fortitude of these intrepid explorers insured that Rabb and his extensive family became an indelible part of Texas history known as The Old Three Hundred. This exclusive group made up the initial 297 Anglo-American families brought south by Stephen F. Austin. For Texans, inclusion in this band is similar in historic importance to having possessed a first-class ticket on the *Mayflower*.

Such incredible feats of spunk, tenacity, and daring should never be minimized. Settlers west of the Mississippi at that time were virtually nonexistent, and the Native Americans of the area didn't particularly care for what they deemed an invasion of sacred land. As a consequence Comanche, Waco, and Tawakoni Indians took turns robbing the hell out of Rabb's extended family and proved especially troublesome for the household of his daughter Rachael Newman and her husband Joseph. The Indians stole horses, cows, corn, pigs, and anything else that wasn't padlocked to a tree or nailed to a wall.

Given the slightest opportunity war-painted Comanche braves took uncommon joy at using the new settlers for bow and arrow practice. Seems that bull's-eye targets and hay bales were scarcer than bird poop in a cuckoo clock. One of their favorite tricks involved waiting until dark, sneaking up on unsuspecting cabin dwellers, and shooting them through the cracks between the rough log walls. It took Texas pioneers a bit, but eventually it came to them that they couldn't leave their candles lit after dark.

The women of the newly established Austin colony often found themselves at the mercy of the wilderness when their men had to be out of pocket. The guys would get hung up a hoopin' and a hollerin' down on the back forty pullin' stumps, or whittlin' and a spittin' over at the McCormick place, or maybe they'd start drinking some kind of locally known tarantula juice and lose track of time. They'd catch the devil from their wives when they came dragging in late smellin' of 01' Spider Killer to find their corncribs, corrals, and cabins burned to a crisp by Indians who used the coals to barbecue all the livestock.

Sarah Jane Newman, hereafter referred to as Sally, probably inherited her strength of character and spirit from her courageous mother Rachael. The term ring-tailed-tooter is totally appropriate when referring to mother Rachael. Legend has it that during one of Joe Newman's frequent absences, Comanches came to the unguarded cabin and

2

*The Lone Star Bar & Billiard Saloon was typical of those in small towns in Texas during the late nineteenth century. This undated and unidentifiable carte-de-visite graphically exposes the "watering holes" of most average folk as being glaringly different from the large saloons and parlour houses of San Antonio, Fort Worth, and Dallas.* Courtesy Texas State Library & Archives Commission

politely asked if they could borrow a cup of scalps. Mrs. Newman took umbrage at such unwanted familiarity and promptly chopped off one of the begging offenders' toes with a double-bit ax while he stood on the front porch. For those readers who harbor an interest in trivia, she used the now famous George Washington double-handed, overhead swing and separated the malefactor from several of his digits with one blow. The injured miscreant's angered friends then tried to enter the home by way of the chimney. A feisty mother Rachael piled feather pillows in the fire grate and set them ablaze. Two-toed Johnny Big Eagle and Jonathan Black Bottom refused to attack the Newman cabin for years afterward.

Early on, the intrepid Sally displayed just how much she genuinely enjoyed these rowdy social activities and how little patience she harbored for those who didn't want to join in on the fun and games. An oft-told tale has it that while entertaining a neighbor, the young girl noticed several relatives of Two-toed Johnny skulking about in the bushes. The

3

neighbor, a spineless man of course, went into a fit of paralytic panic and claimed his gun wouldn't work. The courageous girl snatched the weapon away from the coward and proceeded to do the manly thing herself. Unfortunately history doesn't record whether Sally managed to do as much damage as her ax-wielding mother, but the idea of the high-spirited, dimple-cheeked female-type child standing up to such unimaginable heathen dangers has warmed the hearts of forward-thinking females all over the Southwest for over a hundred fifty years.

In spite of the stalwart settlers' well-earned reputation for self-defense, Indians of other tribes continued to stop over with the Newmans at every opportunity. During one particularly spirited evening of tomahawk practice, cow spearing, and corncrib burning, approximately 200 Waco and Tawakoni folks had a grand ol' time eating the Newman's largest cow and burning everything on the property—except the family cabin.

Just when it looked like the Indians might force the Newmans to join in and have some good ol' Tejas fun or else, a party of volunteers, said to be the precursors of the world-famous Texas Rangers, showed up and saved the day, or night, whichever you prefer. One of those men happened to be none other than Jesse Robinson. He must've cut a memorable figure at the age of twenty-four. Seven-year-old Sally fell madly in love with Jesse and nine years later married him. During those intervening years Robinson became a genuine hero of the Republic. He had fought at San Jacinto, killed the cannoneer manning the center gun of Santa Anna's line of artillery, and stood nearby when the Mexican generalissimo surrendered to Houston. Later he served in Lockhart's company, stuck around for anything that would get him away from home, and didn't leave the service till sometime after 1842.

Eventually, mother Rachael complained to her husband so much about the social visits of Two-toed Johnny and his friends that the Newman clan fled their initial settlement and took up residence approximately fifty miles southeast in the safer climes of the little hamlet of Egypt about ten miles north of Wharton.

The untimely passing of Joseph Newman in 1831 may well have been the impetus that propelled Sally into maturity at age fourteen and marriage two years later. In 1833 Sally's hero of the plains came riding back into her life like Prince Charming, and the two of them got married faster'n a prairie fire with a tailwind. Well, that's not exactly true. They signed something called a *marriage bond* and five years later finally got around to having a ceremony. Historians, who generally don't have a romantic bone in their paper-dry bodies, feel that the wedding only took place out of legal necessity. Every *married* man was allotted a certain amount of property, and the formal ceremony probably finalized Jesse's right to his allotment. So much for romance.

The ecstatically happy couple immediately moved into their palatial hovel on Jesse's land grant near Gonzales. In March of '36 Sally and her two-year-old daughter very likely got caught up in the great Runaway Scrape as citizens fled before the invading armies of Antonio Lopez de Santa Anna.

Other than that minor little irritant, the starry-eyed lovers seemed to have gotten along swimmingly for about ten years. But in 1843 there was obviously trouble in paradise. Jesse Robinson sued for divorce. He called his bride "a great scold, a termagant, and an adulterer." For those like me, who find themselves unfamiliar with the word *termagant,* I hereby supply you with the definition taken directly from the *Webster's New Twentieth Century Dictionary Unabridged Second Edition-Deluxe Color,* page 1883. "Termagant, n, 1. a boisterous, brawling, scolding woman; a shrew; a virago. 2. an imaginary deity supposed by medieval Christians to be worshiped by Moslems and represented as a boisterous, overbearing figure." Now if you need a definition for *virago,* look it up yourself. Suffice it to say the word has something to do with a description of the classic Amazon. I don't know about anyone else, but I can't think of anything worse than being married to a six-foot-tall Amazon termagant.

But for Jesse Robinson, far more shameful than having to deal with a termagant was the charge of adultery. He claimed that Sally kept a lover named Brown in her washhouse, that she had deserted him for the lover as early as 1841 and had absconded with one of their children. I could find nothing in my extensive and detailed research to suggest that the lovers lived in the washhouse. The soap in this opera was only beginning to bubble up.

Sally's counter suit charged Robinson with cruelty and claimed that he'd squandered her inheritance. Keep in mind that this happened over a hundred fifty years ago, although it has a very modern sound about it. She wanted her dowry restored and custody of their two children, nine-year-old Nancy and six-year-old Alfred. The jury split up the property equally but failed to render a verdict on the kids. This oversight proved a thorn in the grubby paws of each of these angry dogs and never resolved itself. The couple's divorce was finalized on March 6, 1843.

Within a heartbeat of the intrepid Jesse's departure from her life, Sally remarried. But it wasn't to "Brown" of washhouse fame. No, the happy bridegroom turned out to be one George H. Scull, a mild-mannered gunsmith who plied his trade for the campers around Austin County. Whether or not Scull might have been living with "Brown" in the washhouse is a matter best left to conjecture. He and his new wife moved back to Egypt and lived on land inherited from her father. And although she married three more times, Sally retained the name Scull or Skull for the rest of her life. She seemed to feel that if you wanted to intimidate people by way of an ominous image, a colorful name didn't hurt.

Barely a year and a half later, Sally's life took a momentous turn. She and her new husband sold everything they owned, including 400 acres of land, all their livestock, his gunsmithing tools, and every piece of farming equipment they could lay hands on. At the same time, Jesse

Robinson filed legal papers that alleged she and Scull had kidnapped Nancy Robinson and refused to give her over for visitation.

Sally packed her remaining clothing and the kids and hotfooted it for New Orleans. Young Nancy and Alfred were summarily deposited in Catholic school. If Sally thought she had her sweet babies hidden from their father, she couldn't have been more mistaken. Ol' Jesse had enough Texas bloodhound left in him to sniff the kids out. And although the man acknowledged Sally's choice of learning institutions as having admirable qualities, he jerked them out of her school and installed them in one of his choosing. Sally immediately and repeatedly reciprocated with similar actions and the age-old *they're my kids, by God* war got going full tilt.

Then, for about five years, Sally Newman Robinson Scull seemed to drop off the face of the earth. In 1849 she popped up briefly in Wharton County court to acknowledge the sale of some property. She also declared herself a single woman. When quizzed on the possible whereabouts of her sweet-natured, mild-mannered hubby, she snapped, "He's dead."

Evidently no one had nerve enough to carry the investigation any farther, and poor ol' Scull passed into the dustbin of history with almost nothing in the way of evidence to give us even a thumbnail image of the man. There does exist some sketchy documentation that Sally might have exaggerated Scull's demise. His "mark" appeared on legal papers executed in North Texas in 1853. The puzzlement lingers and rumors abound.

At this point Sally appeared to be living the life of a rootless nomad. In 1850 she dropped anchor in DeWitt County and lived near Joe Tomlinson, her sister Elizabeth's husband. Two years later she turned up in Banquete, twenty miles west of Corpus Christi, and bought a nice-sized little ranch. She married a man named John Doyle, and they developed her new holdings into a highly successful trade and livestock business.

No mention is made in any of the author's readings as to where she obtained the money for this venture.

Not long after arriving in the area though, she attended a shindig pitched by a fellow named Henry Kinney and was involved in a pistol fight. Witness John S. Ford wrote the following in his memoirs:

*The last incident attracting the writer's attention occurred while he was at Kinney's Tank, wending his way homewards (from the fair). He heard the report of a pistol, raised his eyes, saw a man falling to the ground, and a woman not far from him in the act of lowering a six-shooter. She was a noted character, named Sally Scull, and was famed as a rough fighter, and prudent men did not willingly provoke her in a row. It was understood that she was justifiable in what she did on this occasion; having acted in self defense.*

The shooting took place right in front of numerous bystanders and might well be the reason for her quickly growing reputation for violence. A tourist from Europe named Julius Froebel overheard a report of the gunfight from a group of friendly drunks who claimed to have attended the fair. In his journal published in 1859, he related the following conversation:

*They were speaking of a North American Amazon, a perfect female desperado, who from inclination has chosen for her residence the wild border-country on the Rio Grande. She can handle a revolver and bowie-knife like the most reckless and skillful man; she appears at dances (fandangos) thus armed, and has even shot several men at merry-makings. She carries on the trade of a cattle-dealer, and common carrier. She drives wild horses from the prairie to market, and takes her oxen-wagon, alone, through the ill-reputed country between Corpus Christ and the Rio Grande.*

No doubt about it, ol' Sally must've stuck out like a sore thumb at that point. The entire population of South Texas was said to recognize her as she rambled across the rough land with her mule trains and horse herds. At a time when it was considered unnatural for a woman to wear pants, she preferred to dress in the style of a man. Her favorite fashion statement included a buckskin shirt and *chibarros,* a garment made of rawhide or heavy cotton bloomers tied at the ankles with leather thongs. In cold weather she often sported bright red flannel *chibarros.* Beneath this getup she hid two French pistols on formal occasions, but for everyday wear a gun belt and heavy revolvers worked fine.

A lonely Sally evidently longed to have some family nearby and persuaded her cousin John Rabb and his friend W. W. Wright to move south and acquire land near hers. In 1857 Rabb began running huge herds of cattle under his now famous Bow and Arrow brand and prospered to such a great degree that upon his departure for that vast cattle drive in the sky in 1872, his widow, Martha, enjoyed the affectionate sobriquet of Cattle Queen of Texas.

His buddy W. W. Wright took perverse pleasure at being something of a character. Known as W 6 from his stock brand, he never missed an opportunity for a practical joke. Sally Skull turned out to be one of his favorite targets. She couldn't wait to reciprocate. People who knew them tell a tale of how Sally drew first blood in the jokester contest by swapping ol' W 6 a horse that was blind in one eye. The star-crossed animal stumbled into W 6's cistern and landed headfirst in the ranch's drinking water. Poor beast drowned and left W 6 with the prickly problem of removing the carcass and waiting for enough rain to clear up a serious water pollution problem.

Revenge came sweet and cold when ol' W 6 coaxed a $500 bet out of Sally on a ringer of a horse he entered in a race. The animal looked about one step away from the dog food factory, but crossed the finish line like a bolt of hair-covered, skeletal lightning. The high stakes loss went down as one of the few times Sally Skull made a mistake judging horseflesh. She enjoyed the reputation of being a tough trader who possessed an innate ability with and knowledge of the business.

Most of the time she traveled around the countryside acquiring livestock alone and carried large amounts of gold in a bag hanging from her saddle horn. Concerned family members warned her that such practices could prove deadly. Sally laughed, checked the loads in her pistols, and continued on her way. She bought horses from as far south as Mexico and sold them along the coast all the way to New Orleans. Her two six-shooters and a few well-paid, trail-hardened vaqueros made up her only company along the trade route.

Whispered rumors of horse theft often followed Sally, but no one had grit enough to accuse her openly. Anyone who attempted to inspect or cut her herds was subject to be shot. Cattle ranchers aware of her reputation for violence avoided her holdings when searching for misplaced animals.

Sometime between 1852 and 1855, third hubby John Doyle faded from the scene. Now to have one husband *disappear* at this point in history wouldn't be much of a stretcher to believe. Hey, it was easy to die a hundred fifty years ago. But two vanished husbands? Loose-mouthed neighbors told a pack of wild stories of how she killed at least one of her consorts, and numerous of these fables still survive.

One involved a duel between Sally and the dead husband, usually labeled as either Scull or Doyle. Of course her superior aim won the day, and he lost the contest. Another claimed the couple stayed over in Corpus Christi after indulging in a night of heavy-duty stagger juice consumption and dancing. When the poor, stupid goober of a husband couldn't wake Sally the next morning, he did what any caring and loving married man would do: He doused her with a pitcher of cold water. She snapped out of her dreams, grabbed her pistol, and shot the poor man d.r.t. (dead right there).

But the most amazing rumor of them all involved the luckless husband (Scull or Doyle) trying to load an ox team and wagon onto a ferry. The poor man lost control of the beasts, ran off the end of the barge, and dropped into a torrential river. He, the wagon, and all the animals immediately drowned. When her vaqueros asked if she wanted them to search the banks of the river for the doofus's body, in typical Sally Skull fashion she reportedly replied, "I don't give a damn about the body, but I sure would like to have the $40 in that money belt around it." It's fairly certain that, although she might have wanted to, she didn't kill her fourth husband, Isaiah Wadkins. Her petition for divorce described a physically and mentally abusive union that ended when she abandoned him in 1856 after he beat the tar out of her and dragged her around a sizable portion of South Texas real estate. She also threw in the fact that he conducted adulterous relationships with other women. The jury found for Sally and granted the divorce. They also indicted Wadkins for blatant adultery with a woman named Juanita.

By April of 1861, when the Civil War broke out for sure at Fort Sumter, Sally had been living with her fifth and final husband for over a year. Christoph Horsdorff, at least twenty years her junior, earned the nickname Horsetrough from critics because of his decided lack of desire when it came to any kind of physical activity, especially work that involved horses, cows, farming, ranching, or travel. The surprising part of this relationship lies in the fact that Sally's efforts during that turbulent period of Texas's history were double and triple what they had been at any other chapter of her life. If there'd ever been a time when she probably needed help, those were the years.

She dropped ranching like a red-hot horseshoe and jumped feetfirst into the more profitable business of running cotton from Texas to Mexico and returning with weapons of mass destruction for the Confederacy. Trade along the old Camino Real from Matamoros in Mexico to Alleyton in Texas could only be described as *muy bueno.* Eventually referred to as the Cotton Road, it became one of Dixie's few lifelines to the rest of the world. Her property at Banquete, about midway of the trip, gave her the perfect base of operations for this venture. The tough, experienced Mexican vaqueros quickly became teamsters, and Sally's notoriety prior to the war added to the increasingly legendary status she enjoyed.

But even during this harsh and desperate period, she still maintained close contact with her son and daughter. And although parents all over South Texas used the image of Sally Skull to jerk their offspring back into the hard line of good behavior, there is no existing evidence that she was anything but loving and concerned when it came to any child she ever met.

Here's where things start to get weird. When the war ended, Sally once again dropped from sight. Fires in two courthouses destroyed any record of her during that period, and little exists other than an indictment for perjury in the District Court of Goliad County. A jury quickly found her not guilty, and details of the charge are unknown. By 1867 a suit filed against her in 1859 and continued all the way through the war, had ended with the puzzling note "death of Defendant suggested."

Some said she rode off into the wilderness near Banquete with Horsetrough and that he returned alone. Many believe he killed her for the riches she'd accumulated during her career as a smuggler. A fellow by the name of McDowell made wild claims that he discovered a poorly made grave between the Nueces River and the Rio Grande and when he investigated found her body. Authorities never brought charges against Horsetrough or anyone else. He vacated the premises and remarried in July of 1868.

Legends still persist that she simply abandoned her old stomping grounds and struck out to find a new life. Testimony exists from former citizens of Goliad that they knew her as late as 1870. If rumors of her death were greatly exaggerated and she vanished of her own accord, then she most likely moved in with relatives. None other than J. Frank Dobie wrote of a rancher in El Paso named Alice Stilwell Henderson who worked for years writing the life story of Sally Skull. Mrs. Henderson might have known the crusty old dame and written the story as the old lady dictated it. Unfortunately, like a lot of people during this period, the manuscript disappeared.

At the bottom line it doesn't really matter how Sally Skull departed this earth. Her life of struggle, achievement, defeat, revival, and eventual success in spite of unbelievable odds should be what we take from her story. John Warren Hunter, daddy of noted publisher J. Marvin Hunter of *Frontier Times* fame, once came upon Sally while hoofin' it along the Cotton Road in Lavaca County. He was so impressed he took feather quill in hand and whipped out the following:

> *My visitor was a woman!—I met Sally at Rancho Las Animas near Brownsville, the year before and subsequently had seen her several times in Matamoros, and strange to relate she knew me.—Superbly mounted, wearing a black dress and sunbonnet, sitting as erect as a cavalry officer, with a six-shooter hanging at her belt, complexion once fair but now swarthy from exposure to the sun and weather, with steel-blue eyes that seemed to penetrate the innermost recesses of the soul—this in brief is a hasty outline of my visitor—Sally Skull!*
>
> *Sally Skull spoke Spanish with the fluency of a native, and kept in her employ a number of desperate Mexicans whom she ruled with the iron grasp of a despot. With these she would make long journeys to the Rio Grande where, through questionable*

*methods, she secured large droves of horses. These were driven to Louisiana and sold. This occupation was followed until the breaking out of the Civil War, after which Old Sally fitted out a mule train of several wagons, with Mexican teamsters, and engaged in hauling to the Rio Grande—With all her faults, Sally was never known to betray a friend.*

At a time when sloppy drunkenness, tattoos, and body piercing go for colorful behavior, it would be something of a secret pleasure to have a woman of such power and personality reappear. Think of the stir it would cause when she rode her huge horse into the parking lot of your favorite local mall and stepped down to do a little trading. Would that be a hoot or what?

# CHAPTER 2

———— •◦• ————

# HANG 'ER HIGH
## Chipita Rodriguez

There'll never be any way to know for sure of course, but it's just conceivable that Sally Skull and Chipita Rodriguez could've sat down together and knocked back a few tequilas. South Texas legend has it that Chipita conducted business from a lean-to shack near the village of San Patricio—twenty-five miles west of Corpus Christi—at the same time Sally ran cotton down the old Camino Real to Matamoros and smuggled guns back for the Confederacy.

Virtually nothing that can be definitely identified as remotely resembling fact exists about Josefa Chipita Rodriguez—including her name. Most of what now passes for her biography must be identified as myth, hearsay, and whimsical storytelling. Her life and grisly death would be little remembered, nor often retold, were it not for the long-held belief that she was the first woman *legally* executed in Texas—the word *legally* cannot be overemphasized here. A throng of newspaper writers, television reporters, and other such deep thinkers never miss a chance to remind us of her passing every time another woman *might* be put to death by the vengeful hand of the state of Texas.

Residents of San Patricio started the stories of her phantom appearances immediately after her hanging and claimed that the ghastly specter made the requisite showing when a Fayette County woman died in

15

prison just before she was to be executed right after the end of World War I. Reporters waved her ghostly visage in the faces of readers again in 1951. That year Emma Oliver, a San Antonio prostitute who'd been jailed on four different occasions for murder, was saved from hanging by then governor Allan Shivers. Cancer eventually got ol' Emma in 1963. Talking heads and scribbling writers opened Chipita's grave once more in 1978 when Mary Lou Anderson went on trial for murder. Mary Lou's lawyers did a little dipsy-doodle of a plea bargain that got her off. The real, actual, and internationally reported execution of pickax murderess Karla Faye Tucker caused Chipita's most recent resurrection. Each of these emotional accountings played its part in perpetuating what can only be legitimately described as the *legend* of Chipita Rodriguez.

Contemporaries believed that she came from Mexico with her parents, who got out two steps ahead of the Antonio Lopez de Santa Anna tidal wave, which eventually swept across most of the future Lone Star State. Reports have it that her mother died before the little family crossed the Rio Grande. Pedro Rodriguez is thought to have buried his wife in Mexico, settled in San Patricio with their daughter, and nobly sacrificed his life while fighting off Mexican invaders.

After her father's death Chipita made a meager living providing tacos and a place to sleep for tired travelers. No one should be under the impression she ran something like a modern-day bed-and-breakfast. The poor woman lived and carried on her paltry business in a lean-to shack of sharpened sticks pushed into the ground and held up with more sticks. It had a dirt floor, probably open to the weather on three sides, and was about as far from a five-star hotel as a pig is from having feathers. The primitive shack squatted a few miles north of San Patricio on a sunbaked spot near where the Aransas River and the Camino Real converged. As nearly as can be determined, the taco and bed for hire business provided the ancient woman with her sole means of support.

In August of 1863 a Cotton Road traveler and horse trader named John Savage, who openly dragged $600 worth of gold around in his saddlebags, stayed a night or so at *La Hacienda de la Chipita*. Savage, on a horse-buying expedition for the Confederacy, was last seen alive sleeping on a cot in her lean-to. About a week after his visit with the elderly woman, described as being between sixty and ninety years of age, his seriously ax-murdered body, sewn into a heavy burlap bag, popped up on the banks of the Aransas within spittin' distance of Chipita's humble inn.

Those who found the gruesome sack dumped the remains out on the riverbank and hastily determined Savage had either died of several blows to the head or perhaps from being chopped into about half-a-dozen fairly equal pieces. From the moment the sack was opened, disagreement commenced on virtually every fact surrounding the murder, including who actually found the gory bag. Some said Negro women who worked on the Welder Ranch spotted it while fishing, and others claimed a man named Saunders and his friend Captain Turner discovered the floating corpse. One story sounds as good as the other, and you can choose the one you like most. Anyhow, a few days after Savage's well-butchered body popped up, someone also rescued all the dead man's gold from the bottom of the Nueces just a short distance away.

Discovery of the only possible reason for the murder just didn't matter. Sheriff William Means quickly arrested the old woman and a man named Juan Silvera, under the pretext that they'd sliced and diced Savage for his money and then tried to dispose of the body. Based strictly on circumstantial evidence, itinerant judge Benjamin F. Neal indicted the two accused killers and conducted a lightning-fast trial.

To say the legal proceedings were unconventional doesn't come close to a description of the miscarriage of justice that occurred. When the judge showed up, no jury pool existed. Sheriff Means appointed himself foreman and selected the others who served with him. A goodly number of those were county employees or courthouse officials, and some were accused criminals themselves. In less time than it would take for a road-runner to make dinner out of a rattlesnake, those twelve men and true found Chipita guilty of first-degree murder. Silvera they deemed guilty merely of being an accomplice, a or second-degree murderer. Chipita's only comment during her blisteringly fast prosecution was a repeated, *"No soy culpable."* (I'm not guilty.)

Justice came down on the ancient woman like an anvil dropped from heaven. Based on her advanced age and the questionable nature of the evidence, Judge Means heard an impassioned appeal from the jury for mercy. He listened attentively, promptly refused any compassion, and sentenced the old woman to be hanged "by the neck until dead, dead, dead," thirty-four days later on Friday, November 13, 1863. Her lawyer (name unknown and skill at his profession highly questionable) failed to file for a retrial. Such motions for continuance, though common at the time, evidently weren't thought necessary for people like Chipita.

For a while Sheriff Means kept the old woman at his home in Means-ville. The *New Handbook of Texas* indicates that two attempted lynch-ings took place while she was there but were prevented. Those efforts might explain why she ended up in leg irons, chained to a wall down at the county courthouse.

The fateful day for her execution arrived cold, nasty, and overcast. Reports exist that numerous children of the village took mercy on the old woman and provided her with food and enough in the way of mak-ings to have a cigarette rolled from corn shucks. Local ladies helped her bathe and gave her a new dress.

John Gilpin, the executioner, evidently owned enough rope to accom-plish his task, but lacked a wagon for the condemned woman to stand in for the ceremony. He tried to appropriate a new rig owned by a lady named Betty McCumber. She promptly grabbed up a big chunk of stove wood and gave him an old-fashioned Texas butt-whuppin'. Eventually some of Sheriff Means's toadies showed up and forced Mrs. McCumber to accommodate the hangman's request for transportation.

Such minor delays did little toward avoiding the eventual outcome of the court's decision. Loosed from the chains that held her to the wall, Chipita, iron leggings still locked to her skinny ankles, climbed into the wagon unassisted and seated herself on top of her newly built cypress coffin. Some reported they saw her sitting calmly on the box smoking as the wagon made its way through the little town. A number of local folk followed the rolling gallows to the appointed place of execution and watched as Gilpin selected a likely tree near the Nueces River. Now here's where things start to get weird with this tale. The legend says that Chipita was hanged from a mesquite tree. The story has a nice, real-West sound to it. But a fellow named Klatt, whose family owned the property at the time, swore that it couldn't have been a mesquite tree because there weren't any in the area at the time. Years later when a surveyor asked to be shown the famous hanging tree, he pointed out to his guide that the mesquite he saw wasn't old enough to be the original one. The bark didn't look right for a tree that old! Go figure!

Anyway, back to the execution. Gilpin slipped the knot over her head and whipped the oxen. Unfortunately he'd forgotten a very important part of any good hanging. He'd failed to put a hood over the head of his victim. What followed can't actually be termed a hanging—strangling-by-knotted-rope-while-dangling-from-a-tree-limb is more like it. The ghastly spasms of the old woman's contorted face caused some viewers to faint and others to run from the scene screaming.

When the grisly deed seemed to have reached its awful conclusion, no one sprang from the remaining group of observers to help the hangman remove the body from the limb. Gilpin was forced to pull the supposedly dead woman down by himself and single-handedly shovel out a shallow grave from the tough Texas soil near the tree.

But that's not the worst of it. At least one witness claimed that as the dirt was being thrown onto the coffin, he heard a moan from inside the box. Sweet Jumpin' Jehoshaphat! Falsely accused, hastily tried, poorly executed, and then buried alive! Even worse—no wake! Devout Catholics of the village couldn't imagine anything more sacrilegious or strange. Whispered stories of Chipita's possible retribution from the otherworld began immediately.

Sympathetic residents of San Patricio always claimed that the poor woman went to her gruesome death as a means to protect someone else. Some said her son, who actually committed the murder, and others Juan Silvera, who has over the years been confused with the absentee child who hadn't lived with his mother in years.

Everyone does seem to gleefully agree that Chipita's ghost came back to haunt Juan Silvera till the day he died. She'd covered up for his crime, they said, and kept him from hanging. Now she'd have her revenge even if it came from beyond that horrid grave. We don't have any comments from ol' Juan on this otherworldly matter, but that probably wouldn't keep the ghost story alive, or would it?

The actual scene of Chipita's dreadful death has long since blown away like dust in a South Texas windstorm. It has been claimed that not long after the hanging, lightning struck the infamous tree, and someone chopped it up for firewood. Didn't take long for people to forget the actual location of Chipita's grave without the notorious gallows as a landmark. But the legend lived on, and sightings of her weeping spirit floating along the surface of the Nueces every time another woman comes up for execution still abound.

Back in the 1930s, '40s, and '50s teenagers of the area were reported to hasten home after dark at certain times of the year and head for the house rather than spend time making out in daddy's car. It's hard to imagine what they might have feared. There's no indication Chipita ever harmed anyone other than John Savage, and possibly not even him.

Stories still persist about sightings of Chipita's ghost, but some of those responsible for perpetuating them have actually begun to question the validity of such claims. One reporter even admitted that virtually anything found in local newspapers prior to 1960 had to be considered nothing more than extravagant myth. Any truthful account of the poor woman's fate can only be found in the all-enveloping mists of the past. But, people being what they are, there's little doubt that the next time a woman comes up for her appointment with capital punishment in Texas, we're sure to hear Chipita's ghostly legend repeated again on virtually every radio and television station in the state.

# CHAPTER 3

— ◦•◦ —

# Cathouse Madams
## A Bevy of Shady Ladies

There exists the very real likelihood that had it not been for prostitution, Texas and the modern West would still be little more than a dusty wilderness occupied by buffalo, fat prairie dogs, and American Indians. Few so-called *good women* of the early frontier era harbored any great desire to brave the rigors of being one of those who "tamed" the uncivilized western backwoods. Those plucky ladies who followed their husbands into the hinterlands did so mostly because of a simple but deeply held belief in the sacredness of their marriage vows. Few wanted to abandon their established lives for the excitement generated by the prospect of soul-stealing labor, dangerous childbirth, murder at the hands of native peoples, or early death from lack of medical attention.

But those rootless travelers of the manly persuasion, who lived on the fringes of civilization, always needed women and were willing to pay whatever the tariff required. Female companionship for most of those audacious pioneers who blazed their way into the wilds became a business transaction little different than buying a gun, saddle, boots, or a good horse.

As a direct result, during the last three decades of the nineteenth and for a good part of the early twentieth century, virtually every major town in Texas and the West had a sizable red light district. These well-known areas provided the poor, footsore, wayward explorer with food, relaxation, liquor, gambling, rampant prostitution, and the opportunity for indulgence in that wonderfully loutish behavior eternally favored by a large segment of virtually every male population on the planet.

Eager patrons always knew exactly where to look for the "Tenderloin," "Hell's Half Acre," or the "Devil's Addition" when they hit the dusty streets of any sizable town. The commodity most sought by visitors to these seething monuments to depravity was, of course, female companionship of the sexual type. Streetwalking prostitutes, girls who set themselves up in little one-room shacks called *cribs,* and high-priced hookers who lived in boardinghouses were as common as corn bread and buttermilk.

For cowboys with short arms and deep pockets, streetwalkers would do the dirty deed for as little as twenty-five cents. If you wanted a degree of privacy, crib girls got anywhere from twenty-five cents to a dollar for their favors. And for those with enough money to burn a wet elephant, the girls in houses like those run by El Paso's well-known madams commanded as much as three whole dollars for a little of the ol' slap and tickle.

When the railroads got to the Pass City in 1881, they brought the world with them. Farmers, cowmen, bankers, merchants, and men of the cloth rubbed elbows with gamblers, gunfighters, con artists, madams, and soiled doves. The entire economy seemed geared toward making it possible for men of every shape and description to indulge their most depraved cravings, no matter what that might involve. Any ol' lonesome trail bum heading west knew that El Paso could be depended upon for its well-earned notoriety as a place where you could get anything you wanted and nobody gave a damn what you were doing.

Outright approval of such behavior can be found in the El Paso city charter of 1873. It stated that the city council reserved the authority to do whatever it deemed necessary to *control* "houses of prostitution" and to curb the behavior and punish those who did not practice the trade "as may be defined by ordinance."

Into this yawning chasm of tawdry carnality stepped women like Fat Alice Abbott, whose bulky appearance on the El Paso scene brought the areas' first honest-to-God "boardinghouse." Staffed with experienced women she imported from St. Louis, her two-story, wood frame bordello sported a parlor where the customers met and picked the girls they wanted and six bedrooms where *business* could be transacted. In 1886 Fat Alice took the profits from five years of unbridled wantonness and moved into newer and more sumptuous surroundings a few blocks from her original location.

Etta Clark, who quickly became Ms. Abbott's most ardent competitor, arrived in town about a heartbeat later and opened her home for the needy cowboy a few doors away and across Utah Street. Antagonism between these highly competitive women quickly turned from enviousness and dirty dealings, to stealing one another's best performing girls. Alice went so far as to keep a photo album filled with pictures of customers and enemies and accompanied with suitable captions. She crowned a local saloon keeper as the "King of Texas Longhorns" and slapped a huge red "X" across the crotch of infamous man-killer John Selman. The likeness of Etta Clark carried the ultimate of whorish insults by way of an inscription so politically incorrect for our overly sensitive times that it can't even be reprinted here.

Late one night in April 1886, their relationship deteriorated to the point where Alice huffed across the street to retrieve one of her stolen *femmes de nuite*. When denied entrance to Etta's house, the six-foot madam threw her 300-plus pounds against the door and reduced it to kindling. A slapping contest ensued. The five-foot-tall Etta, who weighed about as much as a good saddle, was no match for her huge attacker. Fat Alice won the ear-boxing match, but as she made her retreat, dragging her unwilling former employee behind, the bruised and battered Etta armed herself with a nickel-plated .44 revolver and gave chase.

The screaming prostitute and the huge madam got about halfway down a set of stairs before Etta fired her first shot. She missed. Fat Alice turned, and Etta's second shot hit her in the left side of her pubic arch. The enormous woman stumbled into the street, collapsed into a rapidly growing pool of blood, and was quickly carried to her bedroom for the uncertain medical attention available at the time. (The next day a local newspaper erroneously and, you have to admit, somewhat humorously reported Fat Alice had been shot in the "public arch.") The attending physician gave the moose-sized madam something short of a fifty-fifty chance, but miracle of miracles she lived in spite of ghastly sanitary conditions, colossal blood loss, and everything else horrible you can imagine. Little Etta Clark's lengthy trial ended in a verdict of not guilty on the grounds of self-defense. The jury deliberated just about long enough for the twelve men on the panel to each throw down one shot of 01' Panther Killer, announce their decision, and get back to their own business.

Everyone has limits when it comes to being insulted, and Fat Alice was *muy* offended by the *El Paso Herald*'s little typographical error. She claimed they did it just to embarrass her, as if such a thing were possible, and threatened to put a hole or three in the hide of *Herald* editor Frank Brady. Rumor has it that Brady immediately sought new and more lucrative opportunities in New Mexico and never so much as returned to El Paso for a visit.

Anyone who thought the shooting ended the feud was sorely mistaken. Alice nursed a heavy-duty grudge, so to speak. Several years later she and some colored cohorts set fire to Etta Clark's place and turned it into a pile of charcoal briquettes. They all went to trial, but the case was eventually dropped due to "lack of incriminating evidence." Etta took a hike farther up Utah Street. She built a three-story, thirty-two-room pleasure palace equipped with a pieanner, organ, Turkish carpets, and the most expensive gilt-laden Victorian furniture money could buy. Many a dust-covered visiting cowboy claimed the inside of the place looked like the Taj Mahal.

When it was all said and done, Little Etta had the last laugh. She'd managed to outlive Fat Alice by twelve years when she passed away at her sister's home in Atlanta, Georgia, on October 28, 1908.

✦

Madam Gypsie Davenport started taking "gentlemen callers" at her place in 1883. She and Fat Alice must have become business buddies, because they jointly filed numerous complaints against their rivals for anything and everything they could think of in the way of petty harassment. Members of the local constabulary tended to ignore Gypsie's charges. They seemed to feel that if a list were made of El Paso whorehouse madams given to lapses of judgment, Ms. Davenport's name would lead all the rest.

Not only did she violate the unwritten code of such ladies by indulging in "venereous assignations" with the boardinghouse visitors herself, but she also seemed to enjoy the practice immensely. Customers, who paid a handsome price for such pleasures with the spirited madam, willingly testified that the evening's entertainment was worth every penny.

However, some of those poor, silly goobers, who dropped sizable amounts of money for the opportunity to ride that particular female tiger, also got caught in Gypsie's nefarious "morning after" racket. She'd drown those lugubrious dolts in her own private concoction of frontier scamper juice spiked with laudanum. Then, whilst they snored most profoundly, she'd replace all the furniture in the room with some old broken-down junk, throw a pile of liquor bottles in the floor, and hit her queasy, head-sore paramour with a grossly overpriced tab for his night of drunkenness and wreckage when he finally made it back to the realm of consciousness. Most of the stupid gomers paid it, and despite black-out memory of the entire experience, bragged to all their friends about the great time they'd had.

———

Another famous madam, named May Palmer, operated a house from 1894 until 1910. Little is known of the lady, because few official complaints were ever made against her. She tends to be best known today for crimson calling cards that read: "Madame Palmer's Gentleman's Club, 309 S. Utah, Bell 142, El Paso, Texas." So few of these cards have survived that they now command enormous prices from collectors of such questionable, but delightful, memorabilia.

———

The best known of all the El Paso madams was the courtly Tillie Howard. Miss Tillie enjoyed the rather dubious title of El Paso's most famous and well-liked provider of female companionship. The grand opening of her initial assault into the play for pay market took place in 1892. She immediately established a well-earned distinction for respectability, sensitivity, and compassionate behavior. In other words she wasn't given to public fistfights, didn't beat her employees in front of their clients, and seldom fired a pistol in the direction of anyone important. And wouldn't you just know, because her carriage house overflowed with cats, the neighborhood kids took to calling the place "Tillie's cat house."

On April 5, 1894, at about 5:00 P.M. Tillie Howard's Parlor House served as the setting for one of the wildest gunfights in El Paso history. Baz Outlaw, a former Texas Ranger—dismissed for a serious drinking habit—and deputy US marshal at the time, came to town to testify as a witness in court. He spent that morning and most of the afternoon ripping around from one dive to the next, and by the time he reached Tillie's had managed to burn considerable brain cells by way of an abundance of cheap whiskey.

For reasons forever lost to history, Outlaw entered a bathroom in the brothel and, while in the midst of doing his business, pulled his pistol and began firing. A panicked Miss Tillie ran into her backyard, whipped out her very own police whistle, and cut loose like she was giving everyone at a sawmill a lunch break. Baz finished whatever he had going in the bathroom, stumbled into the yard, and chased the hysterical, whistle-blowing Tillie around while making threats and generally doing everything he could to prove he'd lost his liquor-saturated mind.

A Texas Ranger named Joe McKidrick heard the yelling and commotion, jumped Tillie's back fence, and tried to stop the disagreement. Outlaw raised his pistol, fired, and blasted two .45 long Colt slugs into McKidrick's brain. Then he walked over to the fallen Ranger and put another one in his back just for good measure. Constable John Selman came running up, stopped on Tillie's porch, and witnessed the back shot. He went to grabbing for his pistol just as Outlaw's next shot whizzed by his ear. Selman, often accused of making a lucky shot, drilled ol' Baz in a spot just over the heart, but that wasn't enough. The drunken gunman put two in the old constable's right leg and made him a cane-using cripple for the rest of his life.

Selman stumbled off to try and staunch the flow from a severed artery while Outlaw staggered into Utah Street and collapsed. Bystanders carried him to the Boss Saloon where he fittingly spent his last few living moments stretched out on the bar. A doctor summoned to the scene could do little but shake his head, and four hours later Baz Outlaw met that big bartender in the sky. Reports have it that just before the end came he sat up and screamed, "Where are my friends?"

After a four-year stint providing for the El Paso male's every carnal need and dodging bullets from the likes of Baz Outlaw, Miss Tillie packed up and moved to South Africa. She continued in the pleasure business and returned to Texas's best known border town some years later carrying a fortune in diamonds. With her hard-earned wealth, she erected (no puns intended here) a luxurious, copper-roofed brothel named the Marlborough Club and personally managed it until her death in 1915.

Needless to say, Miss Tillie's earthly departure elicited deep feelings of grief. Friends and customers gifted with a sense of history understood that an important era had ended. Morality had begun to run rampant, and local chamber of commerce types, along with practitioners of the world's oldest profession, understood that the age of open, hurdy-gurdy sex had ended along with all the economic benefits generated by it.

The blue-blooded and prominent of El Paso paraded through the funeral home to pay their last respects. Tillie'd been gussied up and placed in a six-thousand-dollar coffin originally ordered for a Mexican generalissimo whose family pitched a fit and refused to pay for it when they got the bill. A lawyer friend of Tillie's realized that the undertaker's billing efforts involved doing to the old lady what she'd done for people while living. An appeal to the man's better nature eventually resulted in a much smaller and less costly casket. She was buried in El Paso's Evergreen Cemetery.

— —

The major separating factor between Fannie Porter and every other madam in Texas turned out to be her clientele. She ran a wallet-buster of a bordello in San Antonio that enjoyed being the favorite recreational haunt of Butch Cassidy, the Sundance Kid, and their infamous Train Robbing Syndicate—a term Cassidy used and liked much better than the Wild Bunch. Her boardinghouse, at the corner of San Saba and Durango, sported carpeted floors, fine crystal, ice-cold champagne for selected toney customers, and the best-looking fallen angels in the whole damned country.

Wild Bunch historian James D. Horan described Fannie in fairly unflattering terms. He called her "hard, shrewd," and capable of violent

*San Antonio Madame Fannie Porter was said to be "hard, shrewd" and capable of going toe to toe with lawmen at the drop of a shot glass. Her soft, grandmotherly features and curvaceous figure would likely lead most uninformed viewers of this picture to a totally different assessment.* Courtesy Pinkerton's Inc., Archives behavior even in the presence of law enforcement officers. But the only existing photograph of the lady, possibly taken during an investigation conducted by none other than William Pinkerton himself, shows a proud, elegantly dressed woman with soft features and all the rounded curves favored by men of that era.

A number of women who worked for Fannie garnered a goodly bit of reflected fame because of their contacts with her notorious patrons. None, however, achieved the notoriety of the mystery named Etta Place. Virtually no hard-core, factual information exists as to the actual identity of Ms. Place, and the stories about her early life and eventual demise are numerous enough to comprise several books on their own. Historians seem to know two things for sure about Etta—(1) everything and (2) nothing. Considerably more questions than answers exist about her life and death.

The only undeniable fact about Etta Place, if that was actually her name, can be detected by anyone who has ever seen the picture of her standing next to Harry Longabaugh, aka the Sundance Kid. Compared to most of the women of her supposed profession and time, Etta Place was an extraordinarily good-looking woman, beautiful to the point that when a motion picture made in the 1970s sought to tell the Butch and Sundance story, the director portrayed her as a schoolteacher rather than make any reference to the profession most often attributed to her. (See chapter 9)

If you doubt this author's assessment of frontier female good looks, I commend you to any picture of Belle Starr or Calamity Jane. I don't care what anyone says, Calamity Jane never looked anything like Doris Day, Belle Starr never looked anything like Elizabeth Montgomery, and plastic surgery to accomplish such a feat would have to have been done with a chain saw and a military entrenching tool. Unfortunately, more women of the West at that time looked like Calamity and Belle than the lovely Etta.

*Beautiful prostitute Annie Rogers, who worked for Fannie Porter and could well have been the sister of Etta Place from all appearances, is pictured here with Harvey Logan, a.k.a. Kid Curry, deadliest of the Wild Bunch. She followed the diminutive Groucho Marx look-a-like all over the West.* Courtesy Pinkerton's Inc., Archives

A stable mate and supposed running buddy of Etta's, Annie Rogers took up with Wild Bunch wild man Harvey Logan. Of all the members of Cassidy's crew, Logan, aka Kid Curry, was by far the most vicious and already sported the reputation of a killer of men. Annie, who looked like she could have been Etta's sister, also met Logan while selling her affections in Madam Porter's parlor of joy. She immediately set her cap for the pint-sized, heavily mustachioed Groucho Marx of a gunfighter and seemed to fully expect that he would eventually whisk her away from her sordid situation like a miniature Prince Charming. Annie worked under the eternally optimistic, but erroneous, female belief that, "He'll change, because I love him and want him to." Sorry ladies, it didn't work then, doesn't work now, and it'll never work. Didn't matter one little bit. Annie stuck with ol' Harvey, followed him all over the West, and even wrote tender love letters to the little outlaw when he found himself behind bars. Eventually his life of crime drove a permanent wedge between the dewy-eyed lovers, and after a stretch of her own in a Fort Worth "woman's home," Annie escaped and headed into the fog of historical obscurity.

Legend has it that Madam Fannie Porter threw a big going-away shindig for the Wild Bunch in 1901. The gang immediately scattered to their eventual fates, and Ms. Porter vanished from the San Antonio scene. Some people believe she had lived to be an old woman when an automobile accident took her life many years later.

<hr />

Now at the same time Fannie Porter supplied her brand of frontier fun and frolic for the boys down in San Antonio, a woman named Mary Porter (no relation between the women has ever been found) ran an equally famous sporting house in Hell's Half Acre on Rusk Street in Fort Worth. And although she was arrested over a hundred times between 1893 and 1897, she never spent a single night in jail and counted among her friends some the most famous and influential men in the community.

Girls in her employ, interviewed by local newspapers, often sang her praises for what they deemed a "chance" to do something that would help them make a living. But even if those poor, unfortunate women placed their hands on the scripture and words fell like pearls from their scarlet lips, it should never be forgotten that no matter how high-toned the house might have been, the life of a nineteenth-century prostitute in the Old West was invariably dirty, dangerous, and often downright deadly.

Newspapers of the Dallas–Fort Worth area frequently recited terrible tales of the soiled doves' rootlessness, depression, abuse, suicide, and murder. Those poor women nightly faced the prospect of being beaten, stabbed, shot, or infected with a venereal disease that could end their so-called careers.

One of the most brutal murders of a *femme fatale* ever recorded during this period happened in the Acre shortly after the infamous gunfight between Long Hair Jim Courtright, a former Fort Worth city marshal turned protection racketeer, and Luke Short, a well-known sporting man, part owner of the White Elephant Saloon, and bosom buddy of none other than Bat Masterson. Long Hair Jim's reputation as a dangerous pistolero failed him on the night of February 8, 1887, when he grabbed for one of the two guns on his hips. Short put at least four .45 long Colt slugs into ol' Jim faster'n bunkhouse chili goin' through a crew of cowboys.

About a week later, the lifeless body of a streetwalking lady of the evening and dance hall queen known only as Miss Sally was discovered nailed to the door of an outhouse behind a dance hall where she had tripped the light fantastic the night before. Her brutal crucifixion death might have attracted little attention had it not been for its following so closely on the heels of the uproar surrounding the Courtright–Short pistol party. Lawmen claimed to have found no clues as to who might have been responsible for the murder, and her sad passing remains an enduring mystery, which has been repeated in virtually every book ever written about Fort Worth.

The image that most people have of the beautiful, laughing, back-slapping woman working the crowd in a saloon that looks like the inside of a European music hall turns out to be an invention of imaginative pulp fiction writers and don't-give-a-damn-about-history western movies. For any of the poor girls who worked for Mary Porter to find it possible, after a night of bein' rode hard and put up wet, to say nice things about the politically talented madam is nothing short of amazing. In spite of all that goodwill though, she also had her quota of deeply depressed and desperate ladies of ill fame who committed suicide while working for her.

Much like Miss Tillie Howard, Mary enjoyed the questionable title of being Fort Worth's most "famous" madam, probably because she outlived all the rest of them and has often been confused with her better-known sister of the sheets Fannie in San Antonio. She weathered arrests, trials, fines, bad publicity, gunfire, outbreaks of moral righteousness, and every other negative thing that can be imagined to put a crimp in a cathouse madam's day. But in 1906, while still plying the trade she'd been at for decades, she suddenly died.

During Ms. Porter's reign as "Queen of Fort Worth Madams," her stiffest competition, so to speak, came from Jessie Reeves, who owned a boardinghouse almost directly across the street at the corner of Eleventh and Rusk. Born and raised in Spain, Miss Jessie made it to the states as quickly as she could hop a boat and dabbled in careers as varied as circus performer and limber-fingered, card-shuffling gambler. After making it to Texas, the lady faro player was accused of cheating by an enraged cowboy, who was most likely fuzzy-brained and flannel-mouthed from heavy-duty consumption of stump juice when he pushed away from the table and put a bullet in her chest. A fifteen-month recovery gave her plenty of time to consider other career opportunities, and whorehouse madam must have seemed like a snap after being shot over the fall of a card.

By the early 1880s she and her sister had moved to Fort Worth and lived in a house at Seventh and Main that boasted the city's very first lawn of actual green grass. Such classy touches followed when she moved to her location on Rusk, and it was said that her girls entertained some of the most influential and highly respected men in the community. Unsubstantiated rumors, that have persisted to this day, linked Madam Jessie with one of the city's more prominent founders. Perhaps that relationship explained why frequent fines and other such harassment didn't seem to bother her one little bit.

Her reputation with the surrounding community wasn't all that bad either. In 1888 a roofing materials business across Rusk Street caught fire and threatened to burn down the whole town. The fire department and an army of local citizens fought the blaze while Miss Jessie and her girls trooped back and forth supplying the firefighters with piles of blankets and quilts used by the brave *bomberos* to protect themselves from the inferno. The men were so grateful that when the conflagration threatened Jessie's livelihood, a well-placed barrage from fire hoses saved the house.

After more than a decade of the flesh trade, Jessie Reeves did something so unexpected people still have trouble believing it over a hundred years later. She was said to have been out for a walk one day and stopped in the open doorway of a building where a fire-breathing, Bible-thumping, soul-saving revival was cranked up to full screech. She stood in the street and fell under the spell of a talented minister of the gospel named Burr. Admissions of a life of sin and freely offered salvation resulted in Miss Jessie leaving her disreputable career and working diligently for the rest of her days to save others by telling the sleazy story of her disgusting but titillating life as a whorehouse madam. In 1900 a religious publication called *Rescue and Mission Work* published her tale, and the name Jessie Reeves was soon known all over the country.

Women who practiced Fannie Porter's profession, like Fat Alice, Etta Clark, Gypsie Davenport, Tillie Howard, Mary Porter, and Jessie Reeves, left us with very little in the way of documentary intelligence about their lives. Brief encounters with law enforcement led to snippets of lurid information, and then they generally just disappeared. Very simply put, we don't know much about bawdy house madams and prostitutes because they were inclined to be a fairly secretive lot in spite of the public nature of their work. They tended to appear suddenly where men congregated and vanish just as quickly when the law or circumstances dictated.

Most of the data concerning their behavior exists in records of their court appearances and very little else. Common practice by the holier-than-thous of the age involved arresting all the madams and their girls in an area at the same time, hauling them before the bar of justice *en masse,* leveling heavy-duty fines on everyone in sight, and immediately releasing them all back onto the streets within hours so they could go right back to doing what everyone in law enforcement knew they'd been doing all along.

Within a few years of Mary Porter's disappearance from the Hell's Half Acre milieu, the upright citizens of Fort Worth saw to it that most of the buildings frequented by gamblers, gunfighters, and loose women were torn down, broken up, and hauled away. It could easily be argued that the end of the Old West of Texas frontier legend came with the deaths of women like Fat Alice, Tillie Howard, the Porter girls, and Jessie Reeves, because afterwards nothing was ever the same.

# CHAPTER 4

◦•◦

# THE SITTIN' HENS OF THE CHICKEN RANCH

## Mrs. Swine, Jessie Williams, and Edna Milton

A holler and a half and a few yonders from Sally Skull's ol' stompin' grounds around Egypt you'll find the little community of La Grange, population 3,951. Within twenty years of the arrival of the first settlers in the area, a widder woman named Mrs. Swine made arrangements for several females to undertake the arduous journey from that well-known den of iniquity, New Orleans, and set up house (so to speak) in a hotel near the town's most popular saloon. Even a hundred fifty years ago, hard-nosed businesswomen like Mrs. Swine understood that if you wanted to sell something, you had to put it out where the buyers were most likely to find it. From these humble beginnings grew what could arguably be called the oldest continuously functioning whorehouse in the country.

As *la prima Madame,* Mrs. Swine started a practice of community cooperation with the little town and its lawmen that endured for almost 130 years. She and the painted ladies who worked their magic under her watchful eye met their clients in the hotel foyer and then escorted them upstairs for whatever they required in the way of services. Business rolled along at a pretty brisk pace for about twenty years. Then the Civil War broke out and Mrs. Swine and one of her employees were run out of town for being damned Yankees and traitors to the cause.

It'd be a pretty safe bet that the flesh business continued after the Rebellion, but any records of it have been lost. By the turn of the twentieth century a red light district near the Colorado River took up where Mrs. Swine left off, and there's every indication that a good time could be had down near the water by one and all.

In 1905 Faye Stewart, who called herself Jessie Williams, purchased a house in the area. She picked up the business like Mrs. Swine had personally bequeathed it to her. Town fathers, deacons from local churches, and representatives of law enforcement got preferred treatment, and everyone agreed that Miss Jessie operated the cleanest, most respectable parlor house on the banks of the Colorado. But that didn't keep the good folk of La Grange from getting a case of the sanctimonious heebie-jeebies every so often. During these fits of righteous indignation, they would threaten to run all the riffraff out of town and sometimes actually did it.

Miss Jessie got wind of one such impending crusade, sold off her holdings in town, and headed for the country. She purchased a nice little plot of land outside town that had several houses on it and set up a completely new operation. Two decades later everyone in the area referred to the largest of those houses as the Chicken Ranch for reasons you'll discover later.

By 1915 the East Texas oil boom that provided La Grange with considerable commerce began to wane. Roughnecks and roustabouts moved to more lucrative areas and left an army of idle harlots in their wake. Most of the women headed for the coast where rampant dissolute behavior assured any willing female quick employment. Others trailed after the army of oil field workers, and a few sought employment with Miss Jessie.

Bluebonnets carpeted the country when two refugees from that mass movement popped up on her doorstep. They must have done a heck of a sales job on her, because she installed them in brand-new rooms quickly added to her little three-room house. From that moment till the ranch peaked out with a population of sixteen girls, all construction took place in this same spontaneous, hit-or-miss fashion.

The prettier and more experienced "sisters" quickly taught their bucolic counterparts all the tricks they'd learned while working a more sophisticated clientele. They adopted a kind of naughty but nice persona guaranteed to make their younger customers feel like men of the world and the older guys like randy young rogues. Naturally, the poor, stupid men thought these sweet young things were absolutely wonderful and nigh unto being God-sent angels hiding amongst the live oaks of South Texas.

Miss Jessie, who recognized management potential when she saw it, quickly promoted the new girls into customer relationship positions. They immediately started a letter-writing campaign for Texas doughboys locked in the life or death struggle in the trenches of Europe. The girls baked cookies, mailed copies of local newspapers, knitted clothing, and sealed every delivery with love and kisses. Naturally those mud-covered doughboy cowboys couldn't wait to get that war over and get back home.

Somewhere along the way, the younger of the sisters met an older gentleman who actually bucked tradition. He did the real, honest-to-god Prince-Charming-riding-a-white-horse routine on her. They got married and she became one of San Antonio's most ardent benefactors and supporter of the arts. The other lady stayed on at the house until she died at the incredible age of eighty!

When the 1920s arrived, everything changed. The whole country went on an extended binge characterized by fast cars, powerful hooch, and hot-bodied, freedom-loving women. The rapid growth in the number of automobiles brought a whole new generation to the concrete doorstep of Miss Jessie's country pleasure palace. She quickly added more rooms and more girls to a building that had begun to resemble a maze used by university psychology professors to test the intelligence of rats.

One of the unexpected side effects of that era was the universal acceptance of the flapper. The female population of the entire country cut its hair, smoked, drank, shed its girdles, and danced the black bottom, the shimmy, and the Charleston. For a while a good many cowboys couldn't tell the amateur whores from the pros. As a result, Miss Jessie's girls could ride around town and visit local stores anytime they pleased.

This raft of new customers, who arrived with the advent of the automobile, didn't go unnoticed by Sheriff Will Loessin. Every evening he stopped by and visited with Miss Jessie and her girls for a little coffee and gossip. It didn't take him long to realize that when some men entered the throes of ecstasy they would confess virtually every serious criminal act they had ever committed. Quicker'n double greased lightnin', Sheriff Loessin earned the reputation as a detective *non pareil,* and the girls became an absolutely indispensable tool of local law enforcement.

Meanwhile, Miss Jessie prowled the hallways of her house and controlled all that went on there with a firm hand wrapped around a good-sized length of iron rod. She had absolutely no tolerance for the aberrant behavior brought back from the bawdy houses of Gay Pair-ree by newly experienced farmhands and cowboys.

The occasional abusive client had to be dealt with as quickly as possible, and, as a result, none of the bedroom doors in the house had locks. She'd sneak up to a door and listen for the bizarre sounds generated by wanton imagination that resulted in acts other than straight-up, missionary position original sin. Given sufficient grounds, she'd burst through the door and present the offending customer with a nice little whuppin' at the end of her iron rod. If she considered the chastised pervert's offense egregious enough, he could be banished and not allowed to return.

The great stock market crash of 1929 brought the country's prosperous blowout to a head banging, let's-jump-out-the-window-of-the-32nd-floor halt. No one was spared. Even backcountry cathouses suffered. Miss Jessie lowered her prices, but fewer customers showed up and not many of them had any cash money. The cost of a regular "date" dropped to $1.50, but so few people were buying, she was forced to convert to a barter business. One chicken—one screw! Pretty soon there were chickens everywhere.

The precipitous fall in the price of a little mattress-bangin' whoopee can be attributed almost totally to the general economic situation of the Depression. But the single greatest contributor to the decline came by way of competition from an army of dilettantes who'd turned to prostitution because of difficulty finding jobs. Folks who studied the situation attributed the unparalleled growth of harlotry during this period to the increase of men with little or nothing to do. Seems like you can't beat (u . . . u . . . uh, never mind) a little promiscuous sex to help reestablish your maleness when things aren't going well. And even if you didn't have a chicken, you could usually find one roosted in the trees along any backcountry dirt road.

Well, after years of nothing but mashed 'taters and fried chicken, none other than President Franklin D. Roosevelt sent in the crew that rescued Miss Jessie and the girls. The CCC (Civilian Conservation Corps) built Camp Swift not far from La Grange, and the lack of customers and money quickly disappeared. Then WWII came along and everyone was flush again. The girls baked more cookies, wrote more letters to the soldiers overseas, and happily cared for the needs of those on leave. The soldiers pined for home, and when they came back, the first place they visited was the Chicken Ranch.

Shortly after the Big War ended, the ranch went through several major changes. Miss Jessie, who'd been sidelined by crippling arthritis, took to her bed, and Edna Milton arrived from Oklahoma. Edna managed the day-to-day operation of the business, and when Jessie Williams passed on to that great cathouse in the sky in 1961, Edna purchased the property from the Williams estate for $30,000.

By the time this last big ownership shakeup took place, Edna had already managed to cultivate a good working relationship with Sheriff T. J. Flournoy, a former Texas Ranger elected to office in 1946. Flournoy had a direct telephone hookup to the ranch installed so he didn't have to stop by in person. Every night until her retirement, he'd call Miss Jessie, and they'd rake through the day's gossip. Sometimes she'd use the phone when a rambunctious customer got out of hand and once called ol' Jim to calmly say, "I'm bein' robbed." A couple of Houston bandits got the surprise of their lives. They were still rummaging around in closets when the sheriff strolled in and arrested them.

Years later the United States and the Soviet Union put in a similar communications system between the most powerful leaders in the world in an effort to avert total nuclear destruction. No doubt about it, Jim Flournoy was a man of uncommon vision.

A hard-nosed businesswoman and a capable madam, Edna Milton continued the traditions established by Miss Jessie and Sheriff Jim. She forbade social contact between the girls and residents of town; weekly visits to the doctor and shopping trips took place at the same time; all supplies were purchased from local merchants on a rotating schedule, and she continued to be the town's best-known soft touch.

Edna was twenty-three when she arrived at the Chicken Ranch and thirty-two when she purchased it from Jessie Williams's heirs. She presided over the absolute pinnacle of its importance. All of the fifties, sixties, and even some of the seventies were financially very good for everyone. On many a weekend, visitors had to line up and wait outside.

Students from the University of Texas and Texas A&M drove by for a visit at every opportunity, while flyboys from Bergstrom Air Force Base got delivered in helicopters paid for by the poor, pitiful, overburdened American taxpayer. Those flights carried sixteen men per trip, and sometimes the shuttle ran all night long. It wasn't unusual for the waiting line to run almost all the way around the house.

The cadre of harlots who worked for Miss Edna constantly changed. New girls brought in new customers, and local regulars always made it a point to come by and sample the most recent arrival. But the well-paid house attendants, who usually also worked as maids and cooks, were inclined to be more enduring. They were familiar with the clientele and knew who to admit and who to turn away.

Only clean, sober, white men were allowed entry to the parlor where chairs were placed on both sides of the room. Customers sat on one side and girls on the other like twelve-year-olds attending their first dance. Girls had from five to twenty visitors a day and charged a dollar a minute. Hey, even after handing 75 percent over to Edna for expenses, it wasn't unusual for them to clear $300 a week. In other words approximately $6,000 a week in today's deflated, no gold behind it, cock and bull, monopoly money. From her cut, Edna paid all the necessary taxes, food bills, medical visits, maid service, and laundry bills. Someone in La Grange made a fortune supplying clean towels for the place.

All new employees had to get past Sheriff Jim. They were fingerprinted and photographed like common criminals and given a set of written rules to live by. Violation of any of Miss Edna's rules resulted in immediate expulsion from the ranch and possible arrest.

By 1973 it looked like the fun and games at the Chicken Ranch might go on forever. Oh, an ambitious politician would wake up ever so often with his BVDs in a knot and rant enough to get a few people fired up to try and do something about the place. But for the most part, Miss Edna and the girls stayed out of the spotlight and, when things blew over, went right on doing what everyone knew they did anyhow. Then something awful happened. Its name was Marvin Zindler.

As near as I've been able to determine, anyone in South Texas who claimed they had never heard of the Chicken Ranch in 1973 could easily be labeled a lyin' son-of-Oklahoma. A meddlin' busybody from a Houston TV station who feigned shock and amazement at such shenanigans, Marvin Zindler, ran a week-long exposé on Miss Edna and the girls under the guise of protecting all concerned Texans from the horrors of organized crime. Jim Flournoy was flabbergasted. Miss Edna almost had a stroke.

Unfortunately Governor Dolph Briscoe found the pressure exerted by irate, hard-shell Bible-thumpers from the farthest reaches of Texas too much to deal with and ordered Sheriff Jim to shut the place down. By August 1, 1973, all the girls had left town and the Chicken Ranch had closed its doors forever.

Miss Edna tried to stay in town and even attempted to purchase a house in Sheriff Flournoy's neighborhood. Her down payment was refused. She moved farther east, married, operated restaurants, and even acted as a technical advisor and sometimes actress in the Broadway musical that eventually became the movie *The Best Little Whorehouse in Texas*.

A year after the scandalous events surrounding that horrible debacle, Zindler showed up in La Grange to do a follow-up on the economic impact of his personal crusade. During an interview with Sheriff Jim a "scuffle" ensued. Zindler claimed the sheriff ripped the film out of the station's camera and hit him in the chest, breaking several of his ribs in the process. But no one believes that a little pushin' and shovin' caused the lawsuit that followed. Nope, the thing that really got Zindler's dander up (so to speak) was when Sheriff Jim slapped him on the head and knocked his wig off. And even that might have been forgiven, but the irate lawman jumped right in the middle of the poor defenseless hairpiece with his number 10 Justin cowboy boots and stomped the livin' bejabbers out of it. Horrified cameramen and producers from KTRK fainted dead away. They thought the enraged lawman had taken his anger out on an elderly Pekingese. (Okay, okay, so I made up the part about the faintin' and the little dog.)

In 1977 some enterprising types from Houston bought the old Chicken Ranch and moved it to Dallas where they opened it up as a restaurant. Wouldn't you just know, they served nothing but chicken dishes. Miss Edna acted as hostess for a while, but the place failed miserably and closed up less than a year later. Sheriff Jim retired, and in 1982, when he passed away, the lieutenant governor and over a hundred lawmen came to pay their respects. Miss Edna seems to have finally accomplished the anonymity so often sought by women of her profession. She disappeared several years back and hasn't been seen or heard from since.

Bert Reynolds and Dolly Parton starred in the movie version of the play. One film critic noted that watching them flubber around each other on screen was like watching two overinflated balloons in the Macy's Christmas Day parade bump into one another for two hours. It's a shame someone hasn't been able to write, direct, and film a better rendition of the Chicken Ranch tale. I mean, come on, you gotta admit. It's a fantastic story.

# CHAPTER 5

———•◦•———

# TEXAS'S BIGGEST HARLOT
## Sarah Bowman

It's not outside the realm of believability that Sarah Bowman had more than a handshakin' familiarity with some of the most famous military men of America's nineteenth century. She met them on a beach in South Texas.

In October of 1845 General Zachary Taylor landed an expeditionary force of 3,000 men near Corpus Christi in preparation for the conflict everyone knew would come when Texas achieved statehood. The purpose of this occupation of hotly disputed lands was to make it absolutely clear to Mexico that the United States had determined to keep their newly acquired territory, no matter the cost.

Taylor, elected our twelfth president in November of 1848, counted among his subordinate officers a sizable group of lesser knowns that included Ulysses S. Grant, George B. McClellan, Thomas J. (Stonewall) Jackson, P. G. T. Beauregard, and Robert E. Lee. Our neighbors south of the border were not a bit happy about what they considered an invasion and promised to do the *la cucaracha* on Taylor and his soon-to-be-famous subordinates, given the first opportunity.

A sergeant named Bourjett—an active member of the Seventh Regiment of Infantry—was followed into this bubbling political cauldron by his spitfire of a wife, Sarah. Born in 1813 Sarah Knight Bourjett's first thirty-five years are lost to us, but given her vocation when she arrived on the beach, it's fairly easy to speculate that this was not her first camp follower experience. Gossip had it that she'd been with General Taylor during his Seminole campaign, but Corpus Christi was the first showing that can be proven through eyewitness accounts.

The phrase "camp follower" is nothing more than another euphemism for prostitute. Harlot, soiled dove, lady of the evening, fallen angel, woman of ill fame, camp follower, hooker—they're all the same. Many forget that "hooker," the most commonly used description for these women today, came from General Joe Hooker, who allowed prostitutes free access to his troopers during the Civil War. They soon became known as "Hooker's girls." Eventually patrons of the red light district of Washington, D.C., referred to it as "Hooker's division." Local harlots were called hookers.

When Taylor waded ashore in South Texas, women could not join the armed forces and fight in the trenches except by deceit and disguise. But they could marry a man in the service and enroll with him as a cook or laundress. This allowed them to follow their husbands from battle to battle providing food, clean clothing, companionship, encouragement, and something loosely referred to as "personal services."

The single element that distinguished Sarah from all the other women trailing Taylor's army had to be her size. Big as a skinned moose, she stood six foot, two inches tall and weighed over 200 pounds. That might not sound like much, but the average man in 1845 achieved a height of about five foot, seven inches and weighed less than a 150 pounds soaking wet and holding a big rock in each hand. Fed and ready for market, Sarah Bourjett was *la mujer grande-gigantic.*

Soon after her arrival she adopted the nickname Great Western. Historians believe this title referred to the first steamship to cross the Atlantic in 1838. Probably the biggest thing men could think of to compare her with, the 238-foot-long craft was the *Titanic* of its day. When the

1,320-ton vessel arrived in New York, astonished crowds of spectators lined the docks and gaped in amazement. Evidently the men of Taylor's command were equally stunned with the size and commanding presence of Mrs. Bourjett. A shock of flaming red hair that dropped to her waist and charming good looks only added to their surprise and fascination. The nickname stayed with her, but none of the other six to eight names given her by various husbands and paramours survived for more than a few years at a time.

After an absolutely horrific winter of freezing wind, icy rain, and miserable living conditions, Taylor moved his troops off the beach in March of 1846 and turned south for Matamoros. By now, almost every man in camp knew Sarah. She cooked for Taylor's young officer corps, cleaned their uniforms, and saw to their "comfort" when needed. Her pseudo-military title of "laundress" could never approach a description of the intimate assistance she provided. There was absolutely no way her military record could contain a notation like "biggest, and we do mean biggest, strumpet in the entire, whole and complete army!"

On March 20, 1846, General Taylor halted his forces on the banks of the Colorado River. A Mexican officer on the other side drew a line in the water with his saber and dared the Americans to cross over. Epithets such as *hijo de puta* assaulted the tender ears of Taylor's rugged company. Sarah heard the exchange and detected a certain arrogance in the opposition's curses and pronouncements. Enraged by such impudence, she strode majestically to the water's edge and let all the soldiers within shouting distance know she'd wade the river alone and personally kick every *senor* on the other side's behind till his nose bled. Provoked by such swaggering bravado, the Americans let out a piercing Texas *yeehaw* and charged their adversaries like the devil himself chased them. The Mexicans vamoosed.

This lack of resistance allowed Taylor to push his column all the way to a spot north of Matamoros, where he stopped and had his men build Fort Texas. Sarah, who had purchased her own wagon for the trip, refused to stay behind on the Colorado and joyfully continued her duties under the bleakest of circumstances.

Before the earthen fort could be completely finished, Taylor got word that Mexican forces threatened his supply depot at Point Isabel. He left 500 men under the command of Major Jacob Brown at Fort Texas and rushed back to save the reserves so vital to his continued campaign. The sick, injured, and women were supposed to stay inside the bombproofed areas of the fort and await his return. Sarah ignored the general's order.

The bombardment of Fort Texas commenced on May 3, 1846. Sarah vigorously worked the walls, delivering heavy doses of caffeine and hot meals for the artillerymen. Every day at noon she served up a big bowl of her special *sopa de hudias.* This highly secret bean soup recipe invested the Americans soldiers with such a fearsome enthusiasm for the battle that their rivals spoke of the mixture in tones usually reserved for miracles associated with prominent saints of the church.

The Mexican barrage continued for a week. On a single day more than 1,500 exploding shells thumped and whumped over Sarah's head as she fought, cooked, nursed the wounded, and saw to whatever other needs arose.

On the third day of the siege, the much beloved Major Brown was felled when a single shell exploded almost right on top of his head. He died three days later. The Mexican general, seizing an opportunity to capitalize on the injured major's incapacity, threw another 5,000 men against the walls of Fort Texas. Sarah grabbed a musket and challenged any Mexican to get within rifle range. Shot and shell ripped holes in her artillery cap and ricocheted off the tray she used to deliver meals.

One enemy soldier, who evidently didn't heed her warnings, climbed the walls while she helped load and fire a cannon. He whacked her across the face with a saber, and Sarah shot him deader than Julius Caesar.

General Taylor, who could clearly hear the battle from almost thirty miles away, raced back, saved the day, and renamed the fort for its heroic fallen commander. The Great Western wore the scar left by that Mexican blade like a medal of valor for the rest of her life and earned a new nickname—the Heroine of Fort Brown.

When the army hoofed it for Monterrey, she followed and on arrival set up the first in a series of boardinghouses or hotels she named the American House. Two months later she abandoned that original site, chased her rapidly advancing clientele down, and opened a second such place in Saltillo.

On February 23, 1847, the ubiquitous Antonio Lopez de Santa Anna and 20,000 of his closest personal friends attacked General Zachary Taylor's army of 5,000 a few miles south of a ranch called Hacienda Buena Vista. Texans who fought in the battle testified that Sarah Bourjett's bravery, patriotism, and allegiance contributed greatly to the eventual favorable outcome of a brutal, bloody, and crushing defeat for Santa Anna.

She loaded cartridges, nursed the wounded for Dr. Charles Hitchcock, and even ventured onto the field of battle to save those who could not make it back to the hospital on their own. She berated potential deserters with such caustic language they turned tail and ran back to the front rather than endure her wrath. The all-purpose phrase "son-of-a-bitch" was her favorite term of endearment for those prone to abandon her hero, General Taylor.

Sarah maintained the American House of Saltillo until the end of the war and provided "her boys" with the absolute finest in pleasure for the paltry sum of $2.50. By 1848 Sergeant Bourjett, Bourget, or Bourdette (take your pick) had done a Sally Skull and vanished from the scene. A man named Davis soon replaced the departed husband, and she started to use his last name, which created the impression they were married.

Poor ol' Davis didn't last very long though. Sarah met a man closer to her dreams, and Davis found himself on the outside looking in. We don't know the new beau's name, but he was as big as Sarah and claimed mad love for the woman. 'Course mad love has a tendency to burn out pretty quick, and that's exactly what happened. Evidently she discovered that bigger isn't necessarily better (something us men of the shorter type have tried to tell women for years), and the fiery romance she thought was eternal flared up, died out, smoked, and smelled bad.

When the Treaty of Guadalupe Hidalgo ended the conflict, she drifted away from the army and started moving in the general direction of California on her own. But the Great Western and the Saltillo soldiers managed to cross paths again. She spoke with their commanding officer, a Major Bucker, and requested a position with the men. The rules hadn't changed. All she had to do was find a husband, and her old job as laundress was assured. She rode up and down the line with her skirt hiked up yelling, "Who wants a wife with $15,000 and the biggest leg in Mexico?" What red-blooded American could resist an offer like that? A new hubby jumped from the ranks, and she went right back to her old ways. The poor, unfortunate goober didn't last any longer than the four, five, or six others who preceded him.

Sarah never made it to California. In 1849 she paddled a canoe to El Paso where she became the tent city's first known prostitute/madam. Shortly after her arrival she met an entrepreneur named Benjamin Coons, and the new friends put up the quickly growing town's first real building, a combination eat-sleep-get-your-knife-sharpened sporting house, called the Central Hotel. In about as short a time as it would take you to jerk a grizzly bear's tail, El Paso developed into the favorite haunt of every frontiersman, gambler, cowboy, traveler, and killer of men and animals between Texas and Sutter's Mill. As they used to say in the bawdy house trade, business was a-boomin'.

Her partner resisted the siren call of the goldfields for as long as he could but eventually succumbed and struck out to try and strike it rich. Sarah stayed on and managed their restaurant/boardinghouse until 1850 when she hit the trail again and ended up in New Mexico living with a fellow named Duran and a bunch of kids named Skinner.

Well, that didn't last long either. Quicker'n you could thread a needle on a you-pump-it sewing machine, she married yet another man by the name of Bowman. They hotfooted it to Arizona so fast their moccasins must have been smoking. For over sixteen years it seemed that Albert Bowman was *the man* for Sarah, because both suffered from a serious dose of terminally itchy feet. They moved often and set up business in a number of Arizona and New Mexico locations. She stayed in Fort Yuma longer than any other place in her life. Then she moved to Gila City, Fort Buchanan, and back to Yuma. By 1860 the stalwart but restless Bowman had vanished from the scene with no more fanfare than any of those who came before him.

In December of 1866 this formidable, enterprising, courageous woman died as the result of an insect bite at the age of fifty-three. Described variously as a tarantula, poisonous insect, and poisonous tarantula, it seems inconceivable that so powerful a personality could be brought down by a common pest. Prior to her death she drew a full pension for her service to the country, amassed a considerable estate of cash and property, and upon her passing was carried to her grave at Fort Yuma in a ceremony befitting any fallen military hero.

By 1890 the cemetery at Fort Yuma had deteriorated so badly that the Department of the Army exhumed Sarah Bowman and 158 others. Their remains were moved and reburied at the presidio in San Francisco. It is still possible to visit the grave of Sarah Knight Bourjette, Bourget, Bourdette, Davis, Duran, Bowman, Phillips, and maybe even Foyle.

You don't have to be much of a thinker to draw some remarkable parallels between the lives of Sarah Bowman and Sally Skull. Both met the challenges of their lives head on, head up, and on their own terms. They ventured into frontier places generally reserved for men of the most rugged and hardened types. They fought side-by-side and toe-to-toe with those who shared their sense of adventure and devotion to a freedom not generally bestowed on others of their sex at the time. They owned businesses, amassed considerable fortunes, traveled where they pleased, when they pleased, and with whom they pleased. When they died, few followed who could take their places.

Some might consider it an unfortunate comment on the age we live in today that such women would probably be dragged into the spotlight of video cameras and courts to be prosecuted for conducting their lives in such a fashion. But, hey, they could write a book about their exploits. It'd be a surefire hit, and then we'd know a lot more than we do now.

# CHAPTER 6

━━━━●◆●━━━━

# HELL'S BELLE
## Belle Starr

A woman born in this day and age with a name like Myra Maybelle Shirley would probably grow up and become a country-western singer. All you have to do is close your eyes and you can easily picture her as she struts on stage decked out in faux-cowgirl garb, carrying a guitar as big as a Texas mustang, and topped off with a hat the size of a number 10 washtub.

But in 1848 the diminutive girl of that same name, who would someday be known to the world as Belle Starr, didn't have that many choices. Her parents John and Elizabeth Shirley raised cattle in a still primitive area of Missouri some distance from any town of note. They suffered in many of the same ways as Sally Skull's parents, the Newmans. A bunch of Osage folks liked to pass through every so often and indulge in a little of the old let's-run-these-white-devils-off-our-land game. This heartily enjoyed pastime often involved about as much in the way of looting, pillaging, and scalping as the white intruders could stand.

In 1856 John Shirley gave up on cattle raising in the wilds and moved his family to the relative safety of the thriving metropolis of Carthage, population 100. It might be hard to believe, but he opened, of all things, a hotel. In order to supplement what had to be a fairly sparse business, he also ran a stable with horses and hacks for rent and a little tavern where the unlubricated oiled themselves up before returning to a life of toil and drudgery. It's felt that eight-year-old Belle learned early on how to sing, dance, ride, and care for horses as a result of her father's ventures in the stable and liquor games.

Schoolmates of the time remembered her as clever and intelligent, but possessed of a ferocious personality—a dark-haired little girl who never backed down when confronted with the possibility of fisticuffs with other girls or boys twice her size. Called "May" by family members, her tough, belligerent personality soon earned her a reputation as something of a problem even at that tender time of life.

In her early teens she most likely attended the local finishing school for young ladies. Girls who went to such schools were taught a superficial amount of Latin, Greek, and French, along with everything they could possibly ever want to know about needlework and how to conduct themselves when in the company of their elders and betters. Her father evidently recognized a budding musician when he saw one and coughed up the princely sum of $50-a-year so May could also receive piano lessons.

It didn't take long for Shirley's public house to become a favorite rendezvous for border ruffians and those who sympathized with the Southern cause. Confederate raider William Clarke Quantrill, the James and Younger brothers, and other southern desperadoes visited often. May sang and danced for the tavern's rough clientele and soon became a favorite target for teasing cowboys, wranglers, and drunken yahoos who loved the skinny little spitfire's displays of unparalleled anvil-chompin' temper.

The late 1850s and early 1860s proved a dramatic and dangerous time for anyone living along the Missouri-Kansas border. The slavery issue ripped the two states apart, and the resulting confusion allowed gangs of irregulars led by the likes of Quantrill and Bloody Bill Anderson to rob and murder defenseless citizens with no real fear of being brought to heel.

Numerous stories of young May's exploits for the Southern cause began to circulate as civilization crumbled into the turmoil brought on by indiscriminate robbery and murder. Her skill as a horsewoman helped her in a series of escapades that involved riding through the night to deliver information concerning enemy military movements to Quantrill and his band of ruthless killers. One report credited the girl with an audacious rescue of her brother Ed from the clutches of Union troopers by outperforming the cavalry unit ordered to place him under arrest. Unfortunately, brother Ed still managed to mess around later and get himself killed by them damned Yankees. Some credit her brother's death as the motivation behind May's eventual slide into even more flamboyant behavior and an on-again, off-again career in horse theft and strongarm robbery.

In the summer of 1863 federal troops burned the little hamlet of Carthage, and every farm in the area, to the ground. A few months later, when the victims started to rebuild, they torched it all again. Done on the pretext that the operation would deny the Rebel army and its sympathizers a portion of its supply line, the real effect was to make everyone in the region homeless and turn the entire population into refugees. The Shirley family packed up and struck out for Texas.

Papa John, who loved being called by his nickname "Judge Shirley," purchased a farm about ten miles east of Dallas at Scyene and went into the same hotel-tavern and horse business he'd been so successful with in Missouri. The close-knit Shirley clan quickly made enemies of their neighbors when they drained an essential source of water used by the entire community. They didn't seem to mind much though, because their old Missouri friends Jesse James and Cole Younger stopped by every time heat from pursuing lawmen forced them into hiding.

The rough-and-tumble Texans of Dallas ignored their brothers in Scyene and took a liking to little Belle. She quickly became the most popular entertainer at her father's crude saloon. Her vocal renditions turned the heat up under every cowboy within miles. But Belle's cap had been set for Cole Younger for some time. At age sixteen she fell like a frozen cow dropped from the rafters of daddy's stable in Carthage when the handsome killer cast seductive, brooding, heavy-lidded looks in her direction. Three years later he turned up in Texas, and rumors thicker'n ants on a dead snake spread that Belle was "in the family way" and Cole was the proud daddy. Younger did the manly thing and ran back to the open arms of his gang in Missouri.

Belle wasted no time mooning around and rode off into the night with another cutthroat named Jim Reed, a stagecoach robber suspected in connection with several killings. They hoofed it for a nearby town and were married by a justice of the peace. She claimed later that the marriage took place on horseback and twenty outlaws watched while John Fisher, a well-known Texas bad man, held her horse. No other eyewitness account of this event has ever surfaced.

When Judge Shirley found out about the wedding, he almost popped a major blood vessel in his skull and refused to approve of the ceremony. Testimony exists that her parents spirited Belle away and kept her locked in her room until Jim showed up. He carried her back to his quarters in Rich Hill, Missouri, where a daughter, Rosie Lee, called Rose Pearl, was born two years later. Younger continued to visit the happy couple, which only added fuel to the fire of questions surrounding the child's pedigree. And for reasons no one has ever adequately explained, Rose later changed her last name to Younger.

Authorities eventually got around to charging Jim Reed with murder. The couple ran to the Indian Territories and lived for a time with an outlaw named Tom Starr. When things got too hot for them in the Nations, they fled to Los Angeles. About a year later the murder charges caught up with Reed in California, and they made a beeline back to Texas with their new son Ed in tow. Belle picked up with the nightlife of Dallas, and

Reed went back to his old tricks of robbery, murder, and mayhem with the James, Younger, and Starr gangs.

By the time of her return, Dallas had developed into a busy, wicked cow town full of wild, sinful people. Hey, this was exactly the kind of crowd Belle liked. The population of the bustling city had skyrocketed to about 7,000 permanent souls and thousands of itinerant cowboys, who followed huge herds of longhorns. They all gravitated to the Trinity River area, where the casinos, dance halls, and saloons operated. All Dallas needed was a calliope and an elephant. What they got was Belle Starr.

Little Belle whooped it up. She played and sang in local saloons and drew appreciative crowds who wanted to watch her demonstrate an innate skill at poker and faro. It didn't take long for her side of the table to be stacked with money, and she reveled in her newfound notoriety and self-reliance.

Although numerous tales of Belle's participation in Jim Reed's stick-ups and bloodshed persisted, no one could actually offer up any concrete eyewitness confirmation. But in late November of 1873, Jim, his friend Tom Starr, and Tom's brother Sam waylaid a Creek fellow named Walt Grayson and stole $30,000 in gold from him, which he had in turn pilfered from Creek tribal coffers. Thirty thousand dollars in gold was a lot of money. It'd be the equivalent of about $3 million in the pitiful, depreciated stuff circulating now.

Grayson obviously didn't give that much money up easily.

The thieves found it necessary to apply some considerable persuasion. One story that circulated after the scurrilous act claimed an unknown member of the gang looked suspiciously like a disguised woman.

Newspaper stories once again forced Reed into hiding, but Belle ripped up and down the streets of Dallas on any one of a number of fine racehorses she led back into town immediately following the theft.

"Good folk" were scandalized by her actions and appearance. Her flamboyant velvet riding dresses were accessorized with a hat that sported a gigantic ostrich feather and a cartridge belt around her waist hung with two huge Smith & Wesson pistols. She boldly entered areas usually reserved for men and had no problem strutting into a saloon, standing at the bar, and drinking like nothing was amiss.

When the moon got right and the mood hit her, she changed into buckskins and rode through town like fringed lightning. People on the sidewalks ducked for cover, and local law enforcement ended up lying in the dust like everyone else. She evidently loved the celebrity of being referred to as the "Bandit Queen" in spite of the fact that no warrant had ever been issued for her arrest for anything.

Life in Texas started to go south when Jim robbed the San Antonio-Austin stagecoach in April of 1874. Shortly after the incident authorities arrested Reed, but lack of evidence quickly forced his release. Lawmen suspected Belle as an accessory but failed to act against her for the same reason. A few months later a Paris, Texas, deputy sheriff killed Jim Reed. A *friend* ratted Reed out for the $5,000 bounty posted on his head, and John Morris shot him dead while he was having lunch.

A fanciful story that Belle refused to identify the body in an effort to keep the sheriff from collecting a reward on Reed is probably nothing more than that—a fanciful story. Morris didn't take his blood money and live the life of Riley though. About six weeks after Reed's death, someone shot Morris dead as the devil in a Baptist preacher's front parlor. The killer's identity could not be determined.

Shortly after her husband's untimely passing, Belle dumped her son, Ed, in his grandmother's lap and left little Pearl in the hands of relatives in Arkansas. She returned to Dallas and in 1875 ended up in jail accused of arson in the burning of a store that belonged to a reported enemy. A rancher by the name of Patterson put up $2,400 dollars for her bond. Busybodies in Dallas speculated endlessly about what he got in return.

For several years, rumors persisted that Belle led a gang of thieves and rustlers who stole horses all around the North Texas area. If those stories are true, she had plenty of competition. Reports indicate that upward of 35,000 animals a year disappeared during that period, and at least 700 men roved the range and thickets grabbing whatever they could get their hands on. Reports from the Northwest Texas Stock Association indicated that ranchers had a hard time keeping possession of anything on four legs that wasn't locked in a barn at night.

In 1878 she may or may not have married Cole Younger's cousin Bruce. A mere two weeks after the happy event, if it actually ever took place, someone found his bullet-riddled corpse in a New Mexico cave. A week after that startling discovery, a suspicious record of marriage to Sam Starr showed up in the Cherokee tribal records. Anyway, when 1880 rolled around, it became official and Belle received lawful rights to a share in Starr's Indian lands. At the time, the only way whites could own property in the Nations was through such marriages. Belle reclaimed her children, and the happy family moved to Starr's ranch on the Canadian River, which she promptly named "Younger's Bend." Don't know about anyone else, but if my wife named our home for a former paramour, life could be tough on the range.

For the next few years, Younger's Bend became widely known as a friendly place to seek refuge for horse thieves, cattle rustlers, killers, and anyone else running from the law. Queen Belle held sway over a cadre of men who couldn't read or write and depended on her for pretty much everything they needed in the way of upper level cattle theft management.

But in 1883 her luck began a downhill slide that never stopped. Federal law enforcement types discovered a pair of stolen horses at Younger's Bend, and charges of horse theft were quickly brought against the Starrs in the Western District Court of Arkansas. She and Sam ended up in the dock of no less than Isaac C. Parker, the famous "hanging judge" who'd been given unlimited power to clean up the astonishing amount of criminal activity taking place in the Indian Nations.

Prior to her arrest Belle had gained something of a sympathetic reputation with Judge Parker for what appeared on the surface to be her advocacy of "Indian rights." In actuality this vaguely disguised pretense was nothing more than her way of insuring legal representation for close friends who were widely known as hard cases. She put up bond money and hired lawyers for stellar citizens like the infamous Blue Duck (made even more infamous recently by Larry McMurtry) and cattle rustlers Jim French and Jack Spaniard. Parker liked Belle so much he even appeared as her victim in a Buffalo Bill–style stage robbery put on at a local fair. Reports have it that when Belle stopped the stage at gunpoint and Parker was forced to "stand and deliver," the crowd hooted and cheered for the woman newspapers and novelists quickly dubbed the "Bandit Queen."

Her trial brought on a nineteenth-century media frenzy. As the first woman hauled before the bar in Parker's court, her fame spread far beyond anything she had known before. She took an active part in her own defense, and reporters had a field day speculating on the contents of notes she passed to her lawyers, who appeared to frequently act on their composition. But dime novel fame and a friendly judge couldn't keep her out of jail. Parker sent Belle and lover boy Starr up the river for a year in the federal pen at the Detroit House of Correction.

Sympathetic admirers would have us believe that she turned into "Saint Belle" while in prison. She was said to have spent time writing a book and working diligently with the warden's children like a cloistered nun soon to be nominated for sainthood. There's little doubt she conducted herself as a model prisoner, because she served only six months of her sentence. Poor ol' Sam didn't fare as well. He stayed for the whole year. But when their hot little feet jumped into the stirrups again, they went right back to their old ways.

Trouble between the outlaw lovers reared its ugly head in 1885. Belle took a hike with a murderer named John Middleton, who shortly drowned under what could only be described as questionable circumstances. She knew a threat when she saw one and fogged it back to her hubby amidst rumors that Middleton's swimming deficit might have been caused by Sam Starr standing on the back of the wife-stealing, low-life's neck.

A few days before Christmas in 1886 the lovebirds attended a party. Sam spotted a man who had once served with a posse that ran him to ground for horse theft and decided to start up a friendly little game of let's-shoot-a-bunch-of-holes-in-each-other. Seems that during the chase Sam's horse got rudely murdered, and he could not find it in his heart to forgive the no-account horse-killing weasel. So, he and Frank West pulled pistols at the same time. When the smoke cleared, they'd managed to efficiently and speedily send one another to whatever reward awaited them in the spiritual world.

Dead at twenty-seven, Sam Starr was buried on his ranch at Younger's Bend and faster'n a six-legged jackrabbit, Jim July, a Creek Indian fellow little better than half Belle's age, moved in and changed his name to Jim Starr. About a heartbeat later, deputy marshals from Parker's court were after him for larceny. Belle convinced her child groom it would be best to turn himself in and accompanied the upstanding young man halfway to Fort Smith before turning back to stop at the King Creek store and settle her account.

While paying her $75 tab, she expressed some uneasiness about her current situation to the store owner and his wife, but failed to acquaint them with any specifics that might have shed light on her concerns. A few hours later, on a lonely road next to a neighbor's pigpen, a short distance from her beloved home, someone ambushed the famous "Bandit Queen." Belle's assassin blasted her from the saddle with four barrels of buckshot in the back. Amazingly she survived horrific wounds long enough to speak to daughter Pearl, who barely arrived in time to hear her mother's whispered dying words. Whatever Belle said, Pearl never repeated it.

No one came forward and claimed responsibility for Belle Starr's murder the way Bob Ford bragged about killing Jesse James. Plenty of suspects existed. Most felt a neighbor named Watson did the dirty deed. It was common knowledge that bad blood existed between them. Belle had even threatened to expose Watson as a murderer wanted in Florida. Others draped the mantle of rejected lover on the man, but that's highly unlikely. Their public arguments were widely witnessed, and Watson seldom missed a chance to bad-mouth the woman in or out of her presence.

Some local fence hangers claimed her son, Ed, was the killer. He'd harbored a festering jealousy because of the relationship between Belle and his sister, Pearl. Legend has it that shortly before the murder, mother and son argued over his treatment of one of her prized horses and that she beat the unmerciful stump juice out of him with a horse whip. A doctor named Jesse Mooney allegedly treated the boy's injuries and claimed that young Eddie said he would someday kill Belle for the whipping she had administered. Others held their hands over their mouths and told wild tales of incest between a poor boy and a sadistic mother. True or not, we still don't know to this day who committed the foul and unnatural murder of a woman who'd grown to be a legend in her own time.

Pearl buried her mother in the front yard of the family home at Younger's Bend. Cherokee friends who passed by for a final look and farewell dropped a pinch of cornmeal into the coffin. Dressed in the riding outfit most often seen in famous pictures, she went in the ground clutching her favorite pistol.

As Belle often envisioned, son Ed came to a "bad end." When he was convicted of bootlegging and horse theft, Judge Parker tried to scare him into towing the line with a seven-year jail sentence. It must have had some effect. The warden pardoned Ed as a favor to Parker after a short prison stay. The reckless young man ultimately found employment as a deputy US marshal and died in a drunken shoot-out during an attempt to close a saloon accused of serving poisoned whiskey. Some claim this as evidence of Ed's redemption, others say he was just one of the drunks in the wrong place at the wrong time.

Sister Pearl moved to Fort Smith and took up residence in a well-known "boardinghouse." Evidently she had a talent for the work and soon moved out and opened a place of her own. Like her mother, Pearl married at the drop of a hat. She had four children by a variety of husbands or lovers over the years, took leave of the business in 1918, and passed away quietly in 1925 at the age of fifty-seven.

Shortly after Belle's murder, Richard K. Fox, who published the *National Police Gazette,* put out a twenty-five-cent piece of blatant fiction named *Belle Starr, the Bandit Queen, or the Female Jesse James.* Scores of other books, movies, and even two Broadway plays have added to the extravagant myths attributed to the woman and the times in which she lived. My favorite was a made-for-TV film which starred the remarkably lovely, blond-haired, blue-eyed Elizabeth Montgomery in the title role. Belle must have rolled over in her grave and laughed like a roadrunner with sunstroke at that one. She had once described herself as having a "face like a hatchet." All photographic evidence indicates the woman knew the truth when she saw it. But in the world she inhabited, looks didn't necessarily matter. She possessed something in the way of magnetism, strength of character, and absolute power of personality, which drew certain kinds of men like bees to roses and guaranteed her a place in our shared history like no other woman who ever lived in the Texas that became western legend.

Twenty miles east of Eufaula, Oklahoma, treasure hunters have sifted through almost every grain of earth at the Younger's Bend ranch over the passing years. They haven't found so much as a misplaced horseshoe nail. If she hid a fortune in gold and jewels as legend would have it, either the loot wasn't at her favorite residence, or she was a lot smarter than most potbellied rednecks with metal detectors would like to believe.

There's no indication that anyone's ever had enough nerve to dig up her grave in the hunt for all that loose wealth. 'Course anyone making the attempt would need to remember ol' Hell's Belle might take offense at being disturbed, sit up with that big ol' pistol Pearl put in her hand, and blast holes the size of shot glasses in them. Don't know 'bout anyone else, but I'd pay to see that movie, especially if Ashley Judd got to play the part of Belle Starr.

# CHAPTER 7

———•••———

# THE SHE DEVIL AND
# THE DARK ANGEL

## Beulah Morose

The absolute baddest girl who ever pulled stockings over silken calves has always been the one who could end up getting you killed. John Wesley Hardin's brief but deadly encounter with Helen Beulah Morose serves as a valuable example of that truism. Prior to her appearance in his El Paso law office, she enjoyed the mantle of total obscurity and immediately vanished from history's view with his violent death. Unfortunately for Hardin and almost every other man she came into contact with, Beulah was a walking, talking, living, breathing destroyer of lives the likes of which none of them had ever seen. And scariest of all, the killings she caused happened so far removed from her understanding that none of the men involved recognized brutal death as it approached. Unfortunately, we know virtually nothing of her life before or after the events she helped set in motion during a few lethal months in the year 1859. It is, therefore, necessary to examine her life primarily by way of the reflected circumstances surrounding the men who knew Beulah when fate came for them.

In Bill O'Neal's *Encyclopedia of Western Gunfighters*, John Wesley Hardin occupies the rather heady spot of number two with a bullet in statistics based on how many dead folks he left in his wake and the total number of gunfights he fought. During the almost ten years from 1868 till his capture in 1877, no matter how you sliced it, facing the man with a pistol or any other kind of weapon in your hand usually proved an incredibly stupid thing to do. Very simply put, he might well be one of the most prolific killers who ever walked the dusty streets of the real West.

Hardin started his murderous rip at age fifteen by shooting an ex-slave who wouldn't step aside. He didn't slow down till Rangers captured him in Pensacola, Florida, in 1877. They dragged him back to Comanche, Texas, for trial in the murder of Deputy Sheriff Charles Webb on May 26, 1874. Depending on which source you choose to believe, he'd managed to eliminate eleven, fifteen, nineteen, thirty-one, or maybe even a hundred or so folks, by the time a jury sentenced him to twenty-five years in prison for the *second-degree murder* of officer Webb. They based this highly dubious finding on some rather questionable testimony that Webb drew his pistol first.

Anyway, at the ripe old age of twenty-five, Hardin went to the state penitentiary down at Huntsville, and lo and behold he found God hiding in the corner of his cell. The King James version of the Bible became his favorite reading material, and when he wasn't debating the finer points of metaphysics with other murderers, thieves, and con men, he studied the law. Excerpts from letters to his children at the time tend to lead just about any reader to believe that his nomination to sainthood couldn't be too far in the future.

His writings also indicate he planned to move to a small town upon his release and continue with a career as a practicing lawyer and Sunday school song leader. Sadly, two years before freedom came, his beloved wife died at age thirty-six. Many believe that if not for her untimely death his post prison life might have been upright, respectable, and even law abiding. Hey, it's a tough thing to take, but some people can find good in the worst of the worst, the baddest of the bad, the most evil of the evil.

In February 1894, after fifteen years in the pen, singing hymns and praising God, he won release, moved to Gonzales, passed his test for the bar, and dabbled a bit in local politics. But when the man he supported for sheriff lost a local election, Hardin fogged out of town in a huff and eventually ended up in El Paso where he put up a shingle that announced his availability for hire as a lawyer.

Not much lawyer stuff got done though, because by that time Hardin consumed whiskey of the most dubious quality in titanic proportions. Existing bar bills from the town's more than two dozen saloons indicate his consumption hovered somewhere in the neighborhood of three dollars a day. At the time, whiskey ran about ten cents a shot, as did a glass of beer. Thirty drinks a day in one saloon would tend to render most men comatose. Similar amounts guzzled down in other public houses and bars during the same twenty-four-hour period would seem unimaginable. Such mammoth imbibing doesn't even take into account all the booze bought for him by the groveling crowd of suck-ups who followed John Wesley on his daily parade from one watering hole to the next.

Hardin's meteoric slide into alcoholic oblivion didn't go unnoticed by a local constable named John Selman. Although little known by the general reading public, Selman's biography might be one of the more interesting in the history of the Old West's man-killers. No attempt will be made here at a detailed retelling of his life story, but a cursory examination of the events that led him to the murder of Martin Morose and his ultimate destiny is necessary.

Selman started out farming in Arkansas; moved to Grayson County in North Texas with his family at the age of twenty-one in 1858; enlisted with the Confederacy during the unpleasantness, but deserted; moved to New Mexico after his first marriage and spent several years killing Indians. He was believed to have snuffed the lamp of a local big behaver named Haulph, and counted among his acquaintances Wyatt Earp, Bat Masterson, Doc Holliday, Jesse Evans, Pat Garrett, and Killin' Jim Miller.

For a time, after his wife died in 1878, he stole cattle all over New Mexico and West Texas. Then he worked as a butcher, rancher, and almost anything else he could think of during those periods when he was on the run from the law for one shooting scrape or another.

In 1888 he landed in El Paso with his two sons. After several attempts at ranching and a job in a smelting business, he eventually won election as city constable in 1892. Such crossovers from the shady life of cattle rustler and gunman weren't unusual. Anyone with any brains knew if you wanted to catch a drunk, rustler, or killer, you didn't send a Sunday school teacher to do it. Selman definitely didn't fit the Sunday school teacher pattern.

At about the same time Hardin celebrated his arrival in Selman's town, a two-bit cattle rustler and thug named Martin Morose sold everything he had and vacated the area near modern day Carlsbad, New Mexico, with a posse in hot pursuit. He stopped for about a heartbeat in El Paso and quickly two-stepped it for Juarez just ahead of local lawmen bent on collecting a sizable reward posted for his capture. A few days later a quick-thinking railroad detective recognized Morose's wife, Beulah, when she purchased a ticket for Sonora. With the help of a Mexican policeman, the detective followed her at a discreet distance. After a panting reunion with his wife, Morose was arrested and thrown into prison in Juarez along with his friend and fellow stock thief Vic Queen.

Reports exist that the blond-haired, blue-eyed Beulah didn't take it kindly when Mexican officials slapped the handcuffs on hubby Martin. She tried to pull a pistol on the lawmen but got the weapon all tangled up in her blouse. A helpful passenger on the train managed to jerk it out of her hand before she could put any holes in anyone important. Her quick release after such aggressive behavior demonstrated just how far men would go back then to appear gallant.

As soon as she could hotfoot it back to El Paso, Beulah retained none other than that well-known bad man, barrister, and boozehound John

Wesley Hardin to get her beloved out of the custody of Mexican authorities and force them to return the more than eighteen hundred dollars they'd confiscated when they body searched her shapely person.

By the time the Mexican Supreme Court approved the release of Morose and Vic Queen for lack of evidence, Hardin and Beulah had become close friends. So close in fact that she'd taken up residence in his room and bed. The phrase "personal advisor" took on a whole new meaning.

Beulah, a former prostitute, who'd married Morose in a whorehouse owned by the sheriff of Carlsbad (known as Eddy, New Mexico, at the time), has been repeatedly described by other writers as being something of a looker. The only existing photo of the woman bears glaring testimony to the silliness of such romantic flights of fancy. An ordinary, tired, and manly face stares into the camera as she sits next to a five-year-old child who could not have been fathered by Martin Morose. Little doubt exists, however, that she was clever, possessed an educated mind, could plot and scheme with the best, and given the slightest opportunity would adopt a loud, abusive, and disorderly personality at the drop of a shot glass.

Although she initially tried to maintain the role of dutiful wife by spending a good deal of time near Martin while he languished in prison, her relationship with Hardin soon altered that attitude dramatically. On the advice of her lawyer/lover, she stopped the flow of cash to the jailbird and, after his unconditional release, cut him off completely (so to speak). Sales of jointly held property in New Mexico and cash in hand amounted to a sizable sum of money. Beulah, and by proxy Hardin, ended up with access to all of it. Martin Morose ended up with diddly-squat. Given Hardin's drinking habits and dearth of other clients, Beulah's fortune had to have been a lure impossible for bar squeezins like the drunken gunfighter-turned-lawyer to pass up.

In a quest for revenge, the hapless Morose enlisted the aid of three bold friends, who confronted Hardin while he innocently downed a few dippers of tequila during a visit to Juarez. Newspaper reports said the

*Only known photo of Beulah Morose. The child, though dressed as a boy, is actually a girl. She apparently dressed her daughter as a boy to keep her from being molested.* Courtesy author Leon C. Metz from his private collection

men got "saucy" with the old pistolero. If they thought he'd turn tail and run, they grossly misjudged the man. He smacked Andrew Jackson Lightfoot in the mouth, then pulled his pistol and tried to push the barrel through Lightfoot's stomach into the bar behind him. Still feelin' pretty "saucy" himself, he turned and almost slapped Tom Finnessy's head out into the rutted street. Vaqueros who passed the doorway said the open-handed rap across Finnessy's face sounded like a pistol shot. Both of the fumbling wiseacres were invited outside to put their manhood on display and settle the matter forthwith, but their ears still rang like chapel bells and neither accepted. Vic Queen, the last of Morose's trio of defenders, evidently had some kind of seizure and couldn't speak or move. Smart man.

Well things went downhill from there like a runaway train with a drunken brakeman. Hardin decided that he didn't want to let a prize like

Beulah go back to a loser like Martin (read access to her money in order to keep drinking here), and rather than dirty his lily-white, dice-shootin' hands with another killing, he hired some other folks to do it for him. Must have been the lawyer in him weaselin' its way out.

From this point the story gets pretty confused, but most agree that the killers were El Paso Chief of Police Jeff Milton, Deputy US Marshal George Scarborough, Texas Ranger Frank Mahon (Scarborough's brother-in-law), and Constable John Selman. Seemed like a lot of firepower for a two-bit cow thief like Morose, but Hardin must have wanted the job done right.

The plan was that the four men would split the $1,000 New Mexico reward, plus any cash found on the body, perhaps some extra coins from John Wesley, and he got to keep Beulah.

At midnight on June 29, 1895, George Scarborough baited Morose to the US side of the river with visions of a panting Beulah waiting in the sunflower patch at the end of the old Mexican Central Railroad trestle near El Paso Street. Milton and the other two lawmen-bushwhackers leaped from their hiding places and literally shot Morose to pieces as he hastened toward an expected loving rendezvous with his sweet little wife. Scarborough put at least one .45 slug directly in Martin's middle. When Morose tried to rise in spite of a half-a-dozen wounds, Milton stood on the ambushed man's chest till he stopped moving.

The lovely Beulah and her attorney were the only attendees at the funeral. Everyone with nerve enough to voice an opinion pretty much agreed that Morose did steal some cows now and again, but, they all groused, he didn't deserve to die like a dog in a ditch for it. And besides, they all said, his slide into the grave started when he married a no account, dirty-legged whore like Beulah.

The brutality of the Morose killing so shocked the sensibilities of most El Paso citizens that the district attorney indicted Milton, Scarborough, and Mahon for murder, but all three were acquitted. Hardin and Selman escaped unharmed by the state's need for vengeance, but something about the murder affected John Wesley in the most profound manner. His liquor consumption increased to something approaching the gallon a day level, and his erratic behavior alarmed everyone who had to have contact with the man. On several occasions, at different gambling establishments around town, he accused other players of cheating, scooped up the pot, and simply staggered away. Anyone with grit enough to challenge his acts was issued an invitation to get their pistols and get to work. Evidently no one could muster up the pluck to swap lead with the rheumy-eyed killer, and his life continued on its downhill slide. In one instance the sheriff arrested him but charged the drunken gunman with carrying a weapon rather than accuse him of being a thief. The $25 fine he paid didn't even slow him down.

Demon rum also wrecked whatever relationship existed between him and his lovin' woman. Seems Beulah hit the jug about as often as Hardin. During one of his out-of-town business trips, she got drunker'n a waltzing pissant and tried to push police officer John Selman Jr. (son of the constable) into a pistol fight. He threw her in the calaboose, and it cost her $50 to bond out.

Annie Williams, the lovebirds' landlady, acted as referee at several of their screaming, furniture-throwing, parlor parties. She once burst in on them about a second after Beulah beat Hardin to the draw and threatened to blast him all the way to Juarez and back. It took some fast talking on Mrs. Williams's part to stop what she deemed an impending homicide. Later Beulah even went so far as to confess absolute terror of her devoted paramour to Annie. She blurted out that he'd threatened to kill her on more than one occasion and confessed that Hardin had even forced her to write a suicide note in case he had need of it after he put a few openings in her skull.

You have to give Beulah credit, she recognized that her string had about run out. After an intoxicated Hardin told anyone within earshot that he'd hired the killing of Morose, Beulah packed her bag and hopped a train headed back to New Mexico. No one knows for sure why she checked out, but some suspect she was shocked by the depth of his involvement in her husband's death and the very real prospect he'd do the same for her.

But outside Deming, Beulah had a premonition of Hardin's impending departure from this life and made a hasty trip back. If she thought he might reform and realize what a good woman he had, she was totally wrong. Their fractious relationship didn't get any better, and less than a week after her ill-advised return, she disappeared from the scene again.

Hardin continued to let his mouth get ahead of his alcohol-saturated brain and even implied that he might confess to his involvement in the Morose murder and get right with God. His fellow conspirators evidently didn't take that news well at all. At any rate, on August 19, 1895, John Selman caught Hardin in the Acme Saloon shooting dice and put three .45 long Colt slugs in him. The one that went through his skull killed him deader'n Jesse James.

Various theories exist as to why Selman ended up being the man who punched Hardin's ticket for the hereafter. Around noon on the nineteenth, the sometime friends bumped into one another and exchanged heated words over John Selman Jr.'s arrest of the lovely Beulah. They even tossed threats of bodily harm about as they parted. The story has some nice romantic possibilities to it, but the more probable cause of Selman's antipathy involved a rift between the two killers over shares in loot taken from Morose's bullet-riddled body. Rumor had it that Hardin failed to split the plunder with the older Selman, per their agreement, and the combination of whiskey, foul murder, stolen money, and loose women finally brought their antagonism to a head.

Don't think for a minute that snuffing Hardin's lamp brought *Le Curse de Beulah* to an end. Selman's first trial for Hardin's murder ended in a hung jury, but on April 5, 1896, George Scarborough sent Selman to the Pearly Gates when he dry-gulched the surprised constable in an alley behind the Wigwam Saloon. Seems Selman had let his mouth do a Hardin. He spread it around that Scarborough got paid for Morose's killing, but he didn't. Needless to say, Scarborough didn't appreciate such talk much and managed to put six big ones in Old John Selman. Exactly four years later, almost to the very hour, minute, and second of the anniversary of Selman's murder, Harvey Logan, of Wild Bunch fame, pulled Scarborough up by the roots near San Simon, Arizona.

Beulah did make one last appearance in the Hardin saga. She and the dead gunman's children fought a contentious battle over rights to the manuscript of his autobiography. The former strumpet most likely wrote the bloody opus from Hardin's dictation, and she had the better claim based on a note he left making her a full partner in the project. But, when the case went to court, she lost. The judge very likely ruled against her for a variety of reasons: her former career as a prostitute, the sympathy of the community resided with the Hardin family, and because women had little standing in any Texas court at that time—women of Beulah's repute had none. The verdict still hung in the air like blue-gray gunsmoke when she vanished into the fog of time and contempt.

Fiction writers believe that all good stories begin with change. They introduce new characters in order to stir things up and bring on events that lead to upheaval in the lives they portray. The story of Beulah Morose and Texas's best-known gunfighter reads like fiction. Prolific western historian Leon Metz called John Wesley Hardin Texas's Dark Angel. Somebody needs to hit the keyboard with fingers blazing and turn us out a novel based on these events. Hey, you could title the book *The She Devil and the Dark Angel.* Sounds like a bestseller to me.

# CHAPTER 8

---◦•◦---

## Mistress of the Manor

## Sophia Suttenfield Aughinbaugh Coffee Butt (or Butts) Porter

Forever resting somewhere beneath the murky depths of Lake Texoma lies the site of one of the most famous private homes of North Texas's fabled beginnings. Known as "Glen Eden," the sprawling, white-columned mansion, which once stood there, served as the setting for the area's most celebrated nineteenth-century parties and dances. The mistress of the manor was none other than Sophia Suttenfield Aughinbaugh Coffee Butt (or Butts) Porter. When the end came, many recognized Sophie as a great lady. Her beginnings were far from notable.

Born in the rough frontier community of Fort Wayne, Indiana, in 1815, Sophia was the second child of William and Laura Suttenfield. The army had transferred her father, a common foot soldier at the time, to the crude encampment. When his enlistment ran out a year later, he stayed on in Fort Wayne, built a house, and went into business as a store-keeper, mail carrier, and like Belle Starr's father, a sometimes hotel and tavern owner.

Since we know little more than what you just read about her early years, almost anything added to these scant facts is nothing more than conjecture. But given her later flights of fancy, skill at tall tale telling, and outright lying, we can easily conjure up an imaginative young woman, bored by her raw existence, who lived in the hope of greatness in the future. This single realization makes it easier to understand why so many of the events surrounding her modest beginnings managed to become exalted far beyond any resemblance to reality.

As with other biographical facts of her life, William Suttenfield somehow got elevated in her mind to the rank of colonel and commander of the military detachment at Fort Wayne. Let it never be said that Sophie Suttenfield intended to allow her modest background to get in the way of a glorified future, even if it existed only in her mind's eye.

By the time she reached seventeen, Sophie knew the life of a storekeeper's daughter wasn't for her. For almost four years the dark-haired beauty had constant attention from the post's military men, but those moonstruck soldier boys didn't have any more chance at beautiful Sophie than steers in a packing plant.

Oh, no. She did something we've come to think of as totally twentieth-centuryish. She struck up an affair with, and eventually ran away from home accompanied by, her schoolteacher for crying out loud. Jesse Aughinbaugh, the former headmaster of the local seminary, heard that Mexico was giving land away. He and the lovely Sophie headed south faster than small-town gossip! My sweet lord, the scandal of it all! One can only imagine the shame suffered by her tavern-running father and invisible mother.

This alliance (note the word marriage does not appear here for reasons that will be revealed later) lasted about long enough for Jesse to lay claim to something over four thousand acres of land east of the Trinity River in what is today Houston County, Texas. As she had with her father, Sophie let anyone within hearing distance know that the man of her dreams formerly held high office in the Prussian army and had come to the Americas intent on establishing a prosperous business. Translated into something other than Sophisms, Aughinbaugh turned out to be a German druggist. In other words a storekeeper, like her father.

About two years after their Fort Wayne liaison, Sophie parted company with the man she claimed to have fallen for and eloped with on sight. She kept no diary of the circumstances surrounding Jesse Aughinbaugh's disappearance, and typical of the time, he simply faded from the scene. Close personal friends later reported that her predicament following their separation became so dire that for a time she entered into a career of prostitution in order to survive.

The events of her life got fairly contradictory around this period. She failed to even mention poor ol' Jesse to most of her friends, but told a wild tale about living with a band of refugees caught up in the Runaway Scrape. Since almost everyone in South Texas at that time headed northeast to get away from Santa Anna, her quixotic yarn of being the first woman on the field after the Battle of San Jacinto doesn't make a great deal of geographic sense. But, hey, we're talking Sophisms here, and they're a whole different form of history.

Anyway, she claimed to have personally played the part of nurse to the wounded Sam Houston while death, blood, and gunsmoke still hung in the air over Buffalo Bayou. Unfortunately, Houston made no mention of the lovely Sophie or the quality of her services, whatever they might have actually been, in any of his writings. Those who've speculated about possibly indecorous behavior suppose that Texas's greatest hero might have wanted to keep his sizable Baptist constituency in the dark about any such affair. Numerous scribblers have voiced the theory that the stunningly beautiful Sophia simply followed in her father's and lover's salesman-like footsteps, sold her body when required, and that Houston might have, at some point, been a buyer. Hey, given the time and place, it could've happened.

Whatever the truth of their initial meeting might have been, Sophie and the famed Houston evidently did become close friends. Stories exist that while completing his term as president of the Republic he kept company with the lady now and again. In spite of this relationship, he made no move toward marriage, and Sophie soon began casting about for a better matrimonial prospect.

She set her romantic hook in an adventurous, wealthy, handsome, and well-placed young colonel in the Texian army, named Holland Coffee, who boasted membership in the new nation's House of Representatives. No need to manufacture tall tales about this man's accomplishments. He owned a string of highly successful trading posts where everyone was welcome including the wildest of Indians. More importantly, he also enjoyed a reputation for old, established family wealth. Faster'n a hummingbird's heartbeat, Sophia Suttenfield Aughinbaugh decided she loved Holland Coffee.

However, there was a small problem. Its name was Jesse Aughinbaugh. Seems that neither Sophie nor Jesse had bothered to invalidate their brief marriage if, in fact, they had even been married. Didn't matter. Prospective new hubby Colonel Coffee insisted on something in the way of legally constituted divorce papers before going through with another marriage. Since Aughinbaugh was nowhere to be found, Sophie stormed the Harris County District Court and petitioned for a grant of said divorce, but the legal system went into some kind judicial seizure and forced her to appeal for relief in the recently established Texas Legislature.

After considerable delay and debate, and assisted by some ingenious pressure from Congressman Coffee and his good friend President Houston, the bill of divorcement finally passed on January 15, 1839. Almost exactly a month later, the couple were married at Independence in Washington County. Records exist that indicate Coffee and Sophie had been living together for some time prior to the marriage.

The newlyweds immediately set off on a six-hundred-mile horseback honeymoon and picnic that followed the Old San Antonio Road to Nacogdoches, the Trammel Trace on to Clarksville, and eventually along the Chihuahua Trail to Warren's Trading House on the Red River.

Coffee's fame and popularity led to dances and celebrations at every stop along the way.

By the time they arrived at his trading post at Preston, local settlers had also worked themselves into a party mood and pitched what has been referred to as a "grand ball" in the couple's honor. Just how "grand" a ball could be in such rough circumstances is best left to the tender reader's imagination.

When the eating, drinking, and dancing ended, Sophie and her new husband settled into wedded bliss in their palatial one-hundred-square-foot trading post building described as being more like a fort than a house. From these humble beginnings the pattern for parties and dances at Sophie's home for the next fifty years took form.

For about the first five years of their marriage Sophie lived what can only be described as the roughest kind of existence, but in the process she took on the title of "society queen of the Red River Valley." The home she established for Holland in that tiny ten-by-ten-foot log building contained the most meager of furnishings. Even so, she has been frequently quoted as having said that during that period she was happier than at any other point of her life. Coffee's Trading Post was located near present-day Denison in Grayson County. It sat on a spot overlooking the Red River at a natural crossing place for cattle drovers headed for the railheads in Kansas. In spite of a constantly changing community of cowboys, military types, and other travelers moving back and forth between Texas and the great cattle markets, Sophie probably didn't feel like much of a society grande dame. But then Holland broke the good news that he planned to build her a house befitting a mistress of the manor whose reputation as a frontier hostess of great renown could continue to grow. There's every indication Sophie was overjoyed at such a prospect.

Architectural diagrams of the original "Glen Eden" no longer exist, if they ever did. But given the type of home common at the time it's fairly easy to speculate that the initial version of the biblically titled estate was most likely a single story cabin sporting a central hallway with porches both front and back.

Travelers stopped and visited with the Coffees at every opportunity. As the years passed, Greek columns, larger porches, a second story that housed the master bedroom and guest room, and a wine cellar were added to their frontier palace. Seems Holland fancied himself something of an authority on the spirits of the time. Eventually a coat of white paint got slapped on the whole thing and it took on the look of a Mississippi antebellum plantation house.

Teams of oxen dragged the finest of period furniture from Jefferson, a major port on the Sabine River, to Glen Eden, and Sophie kept several slaves busy planting in the gardens that surrounded the house. When she got everything the way she wanted it, the couple threw a rip-snortin' shindig that lasted for days and cemented her reputation as the reigning social arbiter of North Texas.

The Glen Eden guest lists of the following years read like a "Who's Who" of well-known figures of the time and included frequent visits by Robert E. Lee and future president Ulysses S. Grant. Those fortunate enough to be invited to one of Sophie's soirees rarely declined and were known to happily travel for extended periods over pig trails and bad roads in order see and be seen.

In 1846 Sam Houston made plans for a courthouse dedication in Sherman and intended to stop over for a visit with the Coffees at the same time. But before he could arrive, Charles Galloway, Coffee's nephew by marriage, offended Sophie by reminding everyone in the area of her supposed past relationship with the popular Houston and several other men.

Sophie exploded. She grabbed ol' Holland by the lapels and told him in no uncertain terms that he had to do something about his filthy-mouthed nephew's gossiping ways. Laying on of the horse whip seemed totally in order as far as she was concerned. Holland argued against such action. He felt a fight would do nothing but add fuel to the growing forest fire of hearsay about her shady past. Sophie wouldn't be denied. She heaped aggravation and annoyance on the poor man's head till he felt he had to act.

On October 1, 1846, Holland shoved a bowie knife into his belt, loaded up his six-shooter, a single-shot pistol, and a double-barreled shotgun, and headed for town. Those who witnessed the altercation said that Holland called Galloway out, jumped on the man when he stepped into the street, and seemed resolute in his desire for murder. Unfortunately Galloway had no intention of giving up his life at that moment and skillfully stabbed Coffee to death with his own version of an Arkansas toothpick. In a matter of minutes after the initial dispute, the handsome and gallant Holland was nothing more than an oozing corpse lying in a dirty street.

The community at large universally mourned the death of their famous neighbor, but acquitted Galloway when he came to trial. The jury felt that each man enjoyed the love and respect of his neighbors and both had been swept into murderous action by circumstances beyond their control.

Sophia played the new part of stricken widow to the hilt for a time. She buried Coffee in a huge vault constructed by her slaves from bricks made on the grounds of Glen Eden. Then she sold his business and focused her own efforts toward further enlarging her gardens and running the plantation he'd left to her and her alone. Didn't take too much diggin' in the petunias for Sophie to heed the siren call of New Orleans and some nightlife away from her own extravagant parties and shindigs.

In 1847, during one of her trips to the Crescent City to sell cotton, she met another genuine military hero and prospective bridegroom. A native Virginian, Major George N. Butt (or Butts) was headed for Texas anyway. When the flirting eye of the voluptuous Sophie worked its

*Sophia Suttenfield Aughinbaugh Coffee Butt (or Butts) Porter pictured with third hubby, George N. Butt (or Butts). Her face shows signs of the fading good looks that kept platoons of men and four husbands interested most of her life.* Courtesy Texas State Library & Archives Commission

magic, he shortly found himself chaperoning her back to Glen Eden, where he took up the duties of the departed Holland in more ways than one.

No records have been located indicating that Sophie and Major Butts (the author prefers this rendition of the major's name for obvious reasons) ever marched down the aisle and took the vows. However, according to historians, this relationship turned out to be one of Sophie's better efforts. Major Butts managed Glen Eden so well that its value over a five-year period almost doubled. He was a wine-sippin' party animal who loved Sophie's galas as much as she did, and his southern good looks, manners, and social graces more than complemented her still obvious beauty.

But after fifteen years of seeming happiness and mutual bliss, misfortune reared its ugly head again. In 1863 William Clarke Quantrill and his gang of murderous border thugs moved into Sherman and happily launched into their usual game of let's-beat-the-bejabbers-out-of-everyone, steal-anything-we-can, and murder-those-who-object. Locals, most of whom were Southern sympathizers, initially welcomed the Quantrill bunch, but that didn't last long when the street shootings and general mayhem went unabated.

The beginning of the end came one night at a party Sophie and Butts attended in Sherman. During a particularly spirited dance, shots were fired and knocked tassels off the hat resting on Sophie's beautiful head. An agitated Major Butts confronted Quantrill's men, and a heated argument followed. Seems that the two gun hands had made a bet they could separate Sophie's hat from its decorations and not put any holes in her pretty head in the process. Incensed by such ungentlemanly conduct, the good major gave those responsible a better than average public tongue-lashing.

A short time after the argument, Major Butts made a cotton-selling trip to Sherman and was murdered on the way home by some ambushing lowlifes who turned out to be members of Quantrill's bunch of killers. One of the cheeky butchers even had nerve enough to wear the major's watch while in Sophie's presence. It was a serious mistake in judgment. Sophia Suttenfield Aughinbaugh Coffee Butts incited most of North Texas against Quantrill and enlisted the aid of Confederate general Henry McCulloch in her efforts at retribution. Quantrill and a number of his men ended up under military arrest, but they somehow managed to escape and seek the relative safety of the Indian Nations.

Once again Sophie sought refuge at Glen Eden, and although local Indian tribes looted and stole from her on a fairly regular basis, she enjoyed a great degree of financial security because of Major Butts's past business acumen. At the time of his death, her estate had a value almost three times what they'd originally started with fifteen years before. No matter how you cut it, in 1863 $46,000 was a lot of money.

Major Butts's tragic passing didn't have much effect on Glen Eden party life. Things got back to normal pretty quick, and one of her gatherings precipitated an event that made her well known to all those who loved the South and defended the cause. Confederate colonel James Bourland and his troopers, on their way to Fort Washita, stopped at the plantation for a brief visit. Sophie immediately organized a party in their honor. The good colonel and his grateful men had barely vacated the premises when a squad of Yankees, who had tracked the colonel to her door, showed up. She graciously invited the Northern curs inside, fed them till they could barely walk, and then led everyone into the cellar for a wine-tasting session. Yankees, being their normal loutish selves, guzzled down everything in sight and promptly passed out. Sophie took to horse, swam the Red River, and warned the good colonel a la Paul Revere. Bourland's men returned with Sophie, took the Yankees prisoner, and made her an instant Confederate heroine.

The Indian attacks continued with a vengeance during the Rebellion and eventually forced Sophie to look for a safer place to reside. Sophie hid a fortune of gold coins in buckets covered with tar, headed south, and didn't stop till she reached Waco.

Wouldn't you just know it, she met and married a man there who gave her over twenty years of absolute wedded bliss. In April 1865 Rufus Burleson of Baylor College fame, presided over the marriage of fifty-one-year-old Sophie to James Porter, a former Confederate army officer and judge who returned with her to Glen Eden and restored their fortunes to pre-Civil War levels.

Judge Porter's demise in 1886 left her melancholy and lacking the fire for those social activities that had been so much a part of her life in the past. Time had ravaged her legendary beauty, and men no longer fought for her attention. Hair dye and expensive clothing couldn't restore the past, and in later years she turned her attention to the previously neglected disposition of her immortal soul. Despite several generous donations to the Methodist church, Sophie rarely attended services until Judge Porter assumed room temperature.

At a running, shouting, all glory be to God, come-on-down-here-and-be-saved revival, Sophie pretty much convinced everyone in the congregation of her newly acquired penitent attitude. J. M. Brinkley received her into the sheltering arms of the church and sat beside her bed when she died peacefully in her beloved home on August 27, 1897. A niece of Holland Coffee's and plantation overseer J. H. Williams jointly inherited the estate. Her grave rests near the original site of Glen Eden and is situated between those of Holland Coffee and James Porter.

It would really be great if you could get in your car, drive a little north of Sherman, visit Glen Eden, and walk through the gardens. Or maybe you might stand back and marvel at the edifice like Oak Alley in Louisiana. Sadly, you can't. Back in the forties, the state carefully pulled the original house down board by board, and when Denison Dam closed off the Red River, the original site of Sophie's Tara of North Texas vanished under the waters of Lake Texoma.

Every ancient plank of the manor was numbered like a gigantic jigsaw puzzle. Plans existed to rebuild it above the waterline. The home would be a showplace for the benefit of future generations who could only read of the past and bask in the reflected glory of those who'd gone before them.

But, as so often happens, fate stepped in and put an end to that happy prospect. In a stunning thunderbolt of bad luck, a group of World War II army trainees found that precious stack of lumber on a freezing night and burned the whole thing in order to keep warm! There's nothing left of Glen Eden but the graves. After so much time, fun, effort, and cost, Sophie must be lying in the ground with tears streaming down her cheeks.

# CHAPTER 9

———•◦•———

# A MYSTERY WRAPPED IN AN ENIGMA

## Etta Place

Stalwart readers who've managed to make it this far might remember that the beautiful Etta Place warranted some degree of special note in chapter 3. This writer's belief that Ms. Place occupies a unique spot in the realm of Texas bad girls, or bad girls of the entire West for that matter, remains as timeless and unchangeable as white sand beaches off the coast of Cabo San Lucas, Mexico.

As was stated in the passage mentioned above, Ms. Place suffered from an abundance of good looks in an era when most (please observe I did not say all) of the brave women who followed nasty men west possessed a goodly amount of the physical attractiveness of pack animals. Her fame and the magnificent oak-like mystery that surrounds her identity grew from a single tiny acorn—a supposed wedding announcement portrait taken in New York City at DeYoung Photography Studio shortly before she departed for Argentina with famed Wild Bunch gunman Harry Longabaugh (aka Sundance Kid).

Prior to the discovery of that unforgettable picture by investigators with the Pinkerton Detective Agency, Etta Place did not exist. In the more than one hundred years since the appearance of the stunning face which gazes wistfully into the camera's lens, writers and students of the

West still know next to nothing about her. But the speculation has absolutely no limits.

Now, as nearly as can be legitimately determined, any biographical sketch worth its salt usually begins somewhere in the neighborhood of the date and place where the person being examined managed to enter this life. Well, you can forget about being hit with that neat little tidbit of info. No one—let me repeat that—no one can say with any degree of certainty where Etta Place was born, if she was born, or when. Anyone out there in reader land could take a stack of index cards and write Texas, Missouri, New Mexico, Louisiana, or numerous states back East, on individual cards, blindfold themselves, and throw darts at that flotsam and be about as accurate as those who've authoritatively written on the subject of her origins for the past century.

As a matter of plain fact, no one whose real name was Etta Place might ever have existed. Such a revelation will without doubt fall like thunder on the heads of all true believers in Paul Newman, Robert Redford, Katherine Ross, and Elizabeth Montgomery.

A woman called Etta Place, perhaps twenty-three or twenty-four years of age, surfaced for the first time at Robbers Roost in southwest Utah during October or November of 1896. Prior to this appearance nothing of any substance can be accurately reported about her. How do we know this singularly specific fact about Ms. Place? Because Maude Davis Lay, wife of gang member Elzy Lay and the only other female on the scene at the time, in later life often shared her eyewitness impressions of the beautiful young woman who accompanied Harry Longabaugh into camp that winter. She is reported by surviving family members to have expressed a degree of envy for the stunning beauty and timely fashion sense of someone called Etta Place.

But even that initial showing has generated an endlessly twisting variety of reasons for her being at Robbers Roost, or which of the famous outlaw duo she actually came to share bedrolls with. Maude Lay added to the complexity of whatever relationship existed between the three people with her claim that Etta's visit actually took place in order to further a smoldering relationship with Butch Cassidy that had existed long before she met Sundance. But the consensus on this one seems to be that, we think maybe, or it's fairly certain, as certain as it can be, the Sundance Kid always enjoyed being the object of lovely Etta's affection from the very beginning.

And that's where the Texas connection comes into our little sage-brush romance. Given the crudity of the times and the harshness of the endeavor, women tended to be severely limited as to what they could expect in the way of career opportunities in the West of the late nineteenth and early twentieth centuries.

As has been more than hinted at previously, seamstress, cook, school-teacher, or prostitute headed an extremely short list of ways to keep unattached females in food and a place to live. Of that limited list, the prostitutes tended to make more money and lead, what appeared on the surface at least, much more interesting lives. Since Butch and Sundance often took their vacations from robbery and mayhem in the whorehouses of San Antonio, many feel the Kid met Etta in Fannie Porter's popular and expensive "boardinghouse." They believe this in spite of the fact that no one of her name or description can be definitively traced back to ol' Fannie.

But, hey, since the soiled doves employed by Fannie and others in the Old West side of San Antonio often migrated from as far away as Paris, New Orleans, San Francisco, Boston, or anywhere else in the known world, the possibility that the famous gunman might meet an exceptional young woman of style, beauty, and refinement in such a place isn't as far-fetched as detractors, such as this writer, might want to believe.

For a man like Sundance to recognize uncommon beauty and wish to save it from a fate worse than death goes right to the heart of every man's hormonal upheaval when confronted by amazing female pulchritude.

And on top of that, no less than hardened investigators with the Pinkerton Detective Agency always suspected that the very first encounter between Etta and Sundance took place at Fannie's San Antonio pleasure palace.

The simple truth of the matter has always remained the same—women go where men congregate. And as much as us short, bald, ugly guys hate it, bright, beautiful, educated females tend to be inexplicably drawn to bad boys like Butch and Sundance. It's the age-old "I can change him and make him a better person" trap or crap—take your pick.

When the woman called Etta Place rode away from that 1896 Utah camping trip with Sundance, the fog of time and obscurity enveloped her again. She simply vanished from the face of the earth and didn't reappear until five years later when the couple turned up at the home of his family in Phoenixville, Pennsylvania. To the delight of his sisters, Longabaugh introduced Etta as his wife. He explained his return from the wild and woolly West as being necessary because he had need of specialized medical treatment—before their impending departure to Argentina—for a stubborn gunshot wound to the leg.

Evidently, Etta and Sundance had no illusions about the harsh and lengthy trip facing them and wanted to be completely rested and recuperated before beginning their extended sea and land journey. In January 1901 they entered Dr. Pierce's Invalids Hotel in Buffalo, New York—a facility that specialized in hot baths and holistic remedies for chronic medical problems.

Pierce's closed its doors in 1941, and no hard copy medical records exist which could enlighten us as to the exact reasons for their joint visit. Here too, the speculation is boundless. Venereal disease, old gunshot wounds, rumors of recurring appendix problems for Etta, Harry's well-documented sinus infections, thinning hair, hammer-toe, housewife's knee—you name it—anything works. Afterward they toured Niagara Falls like honeymooners—though no record exists that they ever married—and by early February the handsome couple had landed in New York City awaiting the arrival of Butch Cassidy.

The reunited trio introduced themselves about town as Mr. and Mrs. Harry A. Place and Mrs. Place's brother Jim Ryan—an alias Butch used quite often. Etta and Sundance rented a suite of apartments on stylish West Twelfth Street and signed the register as Ethel and H. A. Place. Varied, complex, and convoluted reasons have been offered up for the surname Place. The most logical seems to be that Harry, who wasn't the sharpest knife in the drawer, chose it because it was his mother's maiden name and thus was easy to remember. No one can adequately explain away why Etta used the sobriquet Ethel, except that—can you imagine— that could have been her real name!

The thing that this author finds most puzzling about the signature of Ethel Place is its crudity. The educational background attributed to Etta by many writers suffers somewhat by the seeming unlettered scrawl that appeared on the hotel register saved by Pinkertons. Given that penmanship was highly prized and widely taught at the time, it would be unforgivable for a schoolmarm to have such atrocious hand-writing. Then again, Sundance could've signed for both of them. But that wouldn't explain why he put her name above his—something a man of his day and time probably would never do. Oh God! Will the mystery never end?

Anyway, sometime between their early February arrival in the Big Apple and the departure of the S.S. *Herminius* for South America on February 20, 1901, they stopped at DeYoung Photography and posed for one of the most famous photos in outlaw history. Sundance holds a top hat in his right hand and wears a coat with tails. Etta, dressed in a chic gown of dark blue or black velvet, sports a tiny lapel watch and the unforgettable countenance of a woman whose beauty would be recognized no matter when she lived. Whatever else might be written about them, you'd have to admit they were a handsome couple.

From this single source arose all the legends that have surrounded the enigmatic Etta Place. Even something so mundane as her choice of jewelry in that picture has produced rampant speculation that Butch Cassidy bought the watch for her at Tiffany's on February 4, 1901. Records do exist that a Mr. James Ryan purchased some kind of watch from the famous jeweler for a little over $40. Whether or not the timepieces are one and the same is anyone's guess, but when it comes to these three people "anyone" will take a guess about everything in their lives at the drop of a publisher's commission check.

For reasons unknown, Etta and Harry proceeded to Argentina alone while Butch hoofed it back to Wagner, Montana, and one final hurrah in the train robbery trade. The fugitive friends met up again in Buenos Aires the following year, and barely three months later Etta and Sundance left Butch on their Patagonian ranch and steamed back to New York City. Homesickness, medical problems, or whatever you can think up resulted in several of these return trips to the states during the period of 1901-1905. Unknown to Etta and Sundance, the Pinkertons had discovered their photo and begun to circulate it all over North and South America.

According to a letter Butch sent to friends back in Utah in August 1902, during Etta and Sundance's absence, he cared little for the loneliness and isolation brought on by sparse knowledge of the local language and 400 hard miles to the nearest railroad or seaport. Such a response to his seclusion shouldn't be considered odd or unusual for a man known for his gregarious nature and seeming need for constant company. His missive also includes the much quoted "our little family of 3" which has given rise to endless theorizing about exactly what he meant.

Historians often use words like "sketchy" to describe available knowledge of the Argentina period. But the word seems most suitable for Butch and Sundance, not Etta. In fact, accounts of her appearance, behavior, relationships, and demeanor are readily available from a variety

*Perhaps the most famous photograph ever taken of an Old West outlaw and his woman was that of Harry Longabaugh/Sundance Kid and the enigma that was Etta Place. Dressed in the finery of a wedding photo, they posed in De Young's Studio in New York City shortly before departure for South America in 1901. Longabaugh holds a top hat in his right hand and Etta sports the watch that has inspired endless speculation.* Courtesy Pinkerton's Inc., Archives of local sources. Neighbors have described her beauty, elegance, skill as a horsewoman and pistol shot, and obvious intellectual superiority to her faux husband and brother.

One Argentine acquaintance, a Scottish immigrant and sheep rancher named John Gardiner, often provided Etta with books, some intellectual stimulation, and evidently fell madly in love with her in the process. He became jealous of Sundance and even referred to him as a "mean low cur" in letters to friends.

Gardiner wasn't alone in his feelings for Etta. Everyone who became acquainted with the three gringos voiced complete agreement about her beauty and outgoing personality. The Americans frequently attended neighboring fandangos and might have drawn some unwanted attention when the beautiful gringa agreed to dance with the territorial governor at one of those parties. A local lawman also fell under her spell and is reported to have sworn he would resign rather than arrest her when the Pinkerton poster, offering a $10,000 dead or alive reward, showed up on his desk. Gardiner evidently rushed to Etta upon learning of the poster and warned her that detectives were closing in.

By 1905 our happy trio of outlaws had abandoned their Cholila Valley ranch for a fugitive life in the wilds of Argentina, Chile, Bolivia, and Peru. Their departure from the ranch must have been difficult. For the first time in any of their lives, lawful enterprises had succeeded, and prosperity seemed just around the corner. Yet Longabaugh reportedly wrote that even though they'd done well, he never wanted to see the little place again.

From this point on their story becomes so confusing as to make it virtually impossible to tell heads from tails about any of it. Adding to the chaos of the situation was another trio of American bandits who were regularly mistaken for Butch, Sundance, and Etta. It appears that a sizable number of North American immigrants flooded the area at about the same time Etta and the boys arrived. Patagonia's close topographical similarity to the American West evidently drew many from the states who still wished for the freedom and space that disappeared as millions of pioneers pushed the wild men aside, planted crops, and grew kids.

Evidence does exist however that our favorite bandits hid themselves in the woods around Lake Cholila near their ranch for about a year before they headed south to a little town named Rio Gallegos. Butch and the Kid are credited with robbing the hamlet's bank of about $100,000 in early 1905. That figure seems more than a little hard to believe given the location of the bank and period of history. At any rate, local law dogs reported the discovery of three horses at a relay point on the bandit's escape route, and a good many writers have used the old "perhaps" word to make the beautiful Etta the unidentified third rider.

A bartender later linked our brigands to the robbery of the Banco de la Nacion in Villa Mercedes, a town hundreds of miles north of Rio Gallegos, on December 19, 1905. Some feel so many stickup artists practiced their trade at the same time that Butch and Sundance got credit for a good many robberies they never did. Villa Mercedes might well have been one of them. It doesn't really matter. For the two years following the Banco de la Nacion theft, almost nothing of any substance is known about their lives except that Butch and the Kid somehow made it to Bolivia, and Etta Place vanished like a Pacific Ocean cloud blowing across the Andes.

On November 6, 1908, most historians agree that either a company of Bolivian cavalry, or four local police officers from el pueblo de la San Vicente, or a herd or irate burros, shot Butch and the Kid to death when they were discovered to be in possession of a stolen mule. *Los bandidos americanos* were quickly buried in unmarked graves in San Vicente's ancient cemetery, and the questions surrounding their demise went

*Widely published John Swartz photo taken in Fort Worth, Texas, that proved to be one of the poorest decisions Butch Cassidy and The Sundance Kid ever made. Prior to this crystal clear image, only descriptions of the gang existed. Standing (l-r) Will Carver and Harvey Logan. Sitting (l-r) Harry Longabaugh/Sundance Kid, Ben Kilpatrick, and Butch Cassidy.* Courtesy Pinkerton's Inc., Archives

unexamined for over twenty years. The truth of the matter was that no one noticed or gave so much as a tinker's damn who they were or what happened to them.

Rumors of prolonged gun battles and suicide arose and have persisted for almost seventy years since the appearance of a 1930 article in *The Elks Magazine,* which formed the basis for the final gunfight portrayed in the Newman-Redford film. The most bizarre tale surrounding their departure from this life places Etta at the scene, pistol in hand, fighting alongside her man and dying with him. Don't know about anyone else, but your humble author has chosen not to place any credence at all in that one.

The simple, unvarnished fact remains that the woman called Etta Place vanished, and researchers have had little luck tracing her movements after she left the Cholila Valley. The most beautiful outlaw who ever lived simply disappeared, and no one—let me repeat that—no one knows what happened to her.

(Note from the author—referred to as author intrusion by old fiction writing types who like to nitpick.)

Some of you out there in reader land might have detected a certain—how shall I put it—personal attachment for this particular bad girl. Well, there's a very specific reason for that.

At the age of fifteen your incredibly talented scribbler fell deeply, passionately, insanely in love with a young woman named Heddy, who bore a stunning physical resemblance to the DeYoung portrait of Etta Place. For about two marvelous weeks in the summer of 1959, Heddy spent most of her waking hours performing all those feminine tricks designed to drive unattached young men to distraction. For a fifteen-year-old boy in 1959, such behavior guaranteed undying, lifelong passion and devotion.

Then she met him and dropped me like a red-hot horseshoe. He was studying for a personalized bunk down at the local prison farm and a life-long career picking peas. Suffice it to say, he got exactly what he wanted when a jury some years later sent him to the pen for life. Seems that in those moments when he wasn't drunk or beating the hell out of Heddy, he spent all his waking hours as a serial rapist. Did that send Heddy running back to my open arms so fast her tennis shoes caught fire? Not stinking likely. Just made her love him more. No, lovely little Heddy suffered from what I have come to call the Etta Complex—beautiful woman loves astonishingly worthless man and willingly suffers mightily because of him for no apparent reason. I've never been able to understand it. But I'm almost certain Etta Place might well have given her life as a direct result of this horrific affliction.

A few months ago, after almost thirty years of not seeing her, I ran into Heddy in the meat department of a Safeway store. Her worthless husband still called prison home. Seems he committed a robbery after his last parole and got sent back up the river. Heddy looked like a thousand-year-old camel and chain-smoked like my grandmother's wood-burning tin stove.

When I look at that photo of Etta Place, I always say a silent prayer of hope that she didn't end up in as bad a situation as Heddy. Us male romantics tend to dream such dreams, you know.

# CHAPTER 10

———•●•———

# NEIGHBORS FROM HELL

## Allen Hill, Dusky, Nance, and Family

On a hot, dusty afternoon in August 1873, gunfire on the boardwalk in front of Donathan, Culton & Tarkington's dry goods store in Littleton's Springs ignited the fuse of an explosion that resulted in the single greatest mass lynching of women in the history of North Texas. The shooting culminated ten years of sordid gossip, heated arguments, call-out gunfights, and terroristic behavior by a family of yellow dog, "Yankee sympathizers" and their outlaw friends.

The frontier community, located about thirty miles northwest of Fort Worth, had—since its founding in 1856—been a quiet, friendly, off-the-beaten-path setting where everyone knew everyone else and their business. Men helped their neighbors and worked closely with one another for the general well-being of their village of between two and three hundred people. Women raised the kids, slaved like pack animals on the farms and ranches, and prayed on Sunday for the safety of their husbands.

Written descriptions of the town—by the descendants of pioneer settlers—would have the reader believe that Littleton's Springs (its name changed to Springtown in 1875 two years after the bloody end to this story) was the closest thing to the Garden of Eden since the glory of creation as described in Genesis. God-fearing farmers and their wives from the states of Mississippi, Alabama, Georgia, and Tennessee had fled the ravages of the Civil War and established themselves to work a rich, sandy soil easily irrigated by twenty-five artesian wells located in the area. These refugee settlers attended church together, drank shoulder to shoulder in one of the town's three saloons, shopped at Tarkington's, got their hair cut at the only barber shop, and traded stories while having their animals tended by the sole blacksmith. Then, in 1863, Allen C. Hill and his family arrived. In less time than it takes a bull to get to a hole in the fence, all hell broke loose.

Hill, his wife Dusky, sons Jack and Allen Jr., and daughters Nancy (sometimes called Nance), Martha, Katherine, Adeline, Eliza, and Belle rolled into town in a dilapidated wagon held together with rawhide straps. They pitched camp outside the tiny community near the wooden bridge over Walnut Creek and immediately gained a reputation for contentious behavior. Both men and women of the noisy pack tended to be reckless in their conduct and vulgar in their language. Initially, the local population greeted the clan's arrival with a degree of enthusiasm. Unfortunately, their efforts at befriending Hill and his crude family were rejected in every instance.

The tight-knit group's belligerent, standoffish behavior did nothing in the way of ingratiating them with established residents. Local gossips didn't miss a beat either. They quickly began whispering behind their hands about the seriously pregnant Nancy and where the child's father might be. After Hill bought property across Walnut Creek and two miles southwest of town, those same meddlers wondered aloud about her child's fate when it failed to make its naturally expected chubby-faced, rosy-cheeked appearance.

From the moment of their arrival, apocryphal stories about Old Man Hill and his antisocial, ill-tempered band spread around the countryside quicker than you could scorch a cotton dress with a flatiron. The genesis of these tales seems to lie with a man named Jim Dunn, the local blacksmith. Dunn—known by everyone in Littleton's Springs as something just short of the kindest, most generous, peaceable soul to walk the surface of the earth—claimed he made what turned out to be a disastrous attempt at befriending the Hills.

Shortly after the maverick crew set up housekeeping on their quickly acquired property, and counter to the wishes of his far more intuitive wife, Dunn carried some fresh baked bread and a pound of butter over to his new neighbor's house and respectfully tapped on the door. Old Man Hill snatched open the door, pistol in hand, started yelling the foulest of curses, and disparagingly referred to his saintly visitor as "reb." When the stunned smithy attempted to present his offering of food, Hill spat a wad of tobacco the size of a Rhode Island Red rooster into it, dumped it on the porch, kicked it into the yard, and stomped back into the house. As the astonished caller made his hasty, befuddled retreat, Dusky Hill burst through the door like a red-eyed, yellow-toothed banshee. She carried a pot of boiling water and repeatedly shouted something like, "Let me scald the rebel bastard, Pa! Let me scald him!"

Whittle and spit meetings conducted around Dunn's anvil heard the story about as often as they could stand it, and, although everyone had a good laugh at the kindly blacksmith's expense, they decided it best to give the Hill tribe plenty of breathing room. This decision proved better than a good idea when one of the local boys attempted to invite Martha Hill to a church social and was confronted by her slobbering, enraged father. Hill threatened to kill the boy and anyone else who made "advances" to his girls.

It didn't take long for most people to realize that the unfriendly yahoo Hills always had money, but no visible means of support. They didn't farm, run cattle, or sell bootleg whiskey. But, when any member of the group charged into town across the arched Walnut Creek bridge, hard cases, men of questionable reputation, tended to accompany them, and money was never a problem. Some citizens reportedly recognized man-killers, pistoleros, horse thieves, and other such undesirables as now walking in their midst. Wanted men, who purchased room and board—and whatever else they might desire from the Hill women—soon swaggered the streets of Littleton's Springs, a community which had no lawman to protect it.

One highly questionable rumor placed noted bandit and gunman Sam Bass in this group. This piece of hearsay tends to appear particularly facetious on its very surface, because, according to Bill O'Neal's wonderful book the *Encyclopedia of Western Gunfighters,* Sam Bass entered this world in July 1851. That singular fact would have made him only thirteen or fourteen years old at the time of these events. Additionally, Bass did not arrive in North Texas from Rosedale, Mississippi, until 1870. He lived and worked in Denton for Sheriff W. E Eagan until 1874 and was described as a "frugal, dependable employee." His career as a bandit and desperado started in 1876, after a failed attempt at mining in Deadwood, Dakota Territory.

Anyway, the Hills, and their disreputable friends—whoever they might or might not have been—frequently rode into town, fired their pistols at will, got good and drunk at one of the saloons, and thundered off to the family's farm for a night of fiddle playing, dancing, and carousing. Naturally, the dancing failed to pass the good/bad test of nattering fence hangers. Those terrible Hill gals did that "nasty" high-kicking, belly-rubbing kind of dancing so hated by folks who considered themselves "good people." Everyone knew such hedonistic conduct was the same as having "relations" in public.

After about a year's worth of this kind of behavior, things came to an ugly, blood-spattered head as the result of a practical joke played by a man named Ben Morrel. A number of folks had openly complained they'd recently had problems keeping wood for their cook stoves. Some blamed the thievery on unseen Indians skulking around in the bushes.

*Sam Bass has been identified as the man with the large "X" underneath in this photo. Jim Murphy on his right would later betray Bass. The famous outlaw's closest friend, Seaborn Barnes, stands on his left. Springtown legend placed Bass in the company of some of the Hill women and their belligerent bunch, but history fails to support the story. No photos exist of Allen Hill, his wife Dusky, daughter Nance, or the other Hill women.* Courtesy Texas State Library & Archives Commission

Morrel spiked some of his firewood with gunpowder, and a few days later one of his "firecrackers" exploded in the Hills' stove. The blast from a few sticks of seeded kindling rumbled across two miles of Texas and rattled the town. At least that's what second- and third-hand reports would lead us to believe. Such an explosion should have leveled the Hills' rustic backwoods cabin, but no mention of that tragic eventuality exists in currently available records.

So, just about a heartbeat after the smoke cleared, an angry, drunken Allen Hill stumbled into the Star Saloon armed to the teeth and looking for a fight. The only other customer in attendance that day was a one-legged hero of the Confederacy named Bob Peterson. Peterson, who had been sent home to recover after a battlefield amputation, stood a few feet away from Hill and attempted to enjoy his beer and the conversation of a friendly bartender.

The barkeep, whose name is totally—and conveniently—lost in the mists of time, is said to have later reported that the incensed Hill started at one end of the counter, but moved so close to Peterson that the crippled hero hobbled away and took up a remoter spot. Hill followed, then slapped Peterson's beer out of his hand. When the former soldier refused to defend himself, his red-faced antagonist kicked the poor man's crutch and sent it rattling across the room. The smart-mouthed, big-behaver then issued a challenge for the crippled war hero to step outside and get to work with his pistol.

Ol' Bob retrieved his crutch, hobbled into the street behind Hill, still refusing to be drawn into a shooting match, and attempted to leave the scene. That lowlife, scum-sucking son-of-the-north shot the sainted Peterson in the back. As the old soldier went down, he drew his own gun, turned, and put three pistol balls in Hill's black heart. Witnesses said you could have covered those bullet holes with a ten-dollar gold piece.

Family members retrieved the wounded Peterson and eventually nursed him back to health. Dusky Hill and her son Jack claimed the old man's body. Jack spent a goodly amount of his time in town that day berating everyone he could lay his tongue to for his father's death and swore bloody vengeance. Needless to say, most people thought the situation would get better with Old Man Hill's passing. They couldn't have been more wrong.

Son Jack assumed command of the family. Over the next several years, their neighbors came to feel that he and the Hill girls, led by the heavily armed Nancy, headed a fairly sizable ring of horse and cattle thieves. Thundering raids on the town became commonplace. Anytime large numbers of horses boomed across Walnut Creek, everyone scattered and tried to find cover. Locals were pistol-whipped on the streets. Merchants didn't know from one day to the next how much of their stock would be stolen. Some families had their homes burned, and the violence spread to the surrounding counties of Jack, Wise, and Montague. On a number of occasions, lawmen from other parts of the state questioned the Hills and searched their cabin and parts of the property surrounding it. They never discovered anything in the way of condemning evidence, and the lawlessness continued.

The circumstances of Jack Hill's demise sound suspiciously like those surrounding his father's end. In 1870 a gentleman named Aaron Bloomer, a resident of Palo Pinto County, punched Jack's ticket in another call-out gunfight. People in Littleton's Springs hit their knees and said a silent "thank-you Jesus" for what they perceived as deliverance from a punishing evil.

But if anyone really believed the black clouds had parted and the warm glow of pre-Hill family days was upon them, Nancy Hill snuffed those feelings like a coal-oil lamp blown out by a cyclone. Shortly after her ascension to family leadership, the local doctor's twin daughters announced their coming marriage to the brothers McQuade. Virtually every man, woman, and child in town helped in the decoration of a church they'd all pitched in to build. The beautifully prepared brides marched down each side of the congregation, accompanied by their attendants. As they took their sacred spots before the altar, Nance, her sisters, and some twenty others of the Hill gang rode their horses around the rustic house of worship like marauding Indians. When the gunfire finally stopped, not a single window in the little country church had survived. Fortunately no one managed to get shot, but Nancy's reputation for reckless and dangerous behavior was forever sealed by the incident.

Over the years since the Hill clan's notorious arrival, she had managed to acquire a reputation equal to or worse than her father's or brother Jack's. She'd been obviously pregnant at least twice, and neither baby was ever seen. One of the most horrific stories passed down over the years about the pregnant Nancy's cold-blooded behavior involved her stopping along the owl hoot trail while being hotly pursued by lawmen. She supposedly headed for the bushes, gave birth to one of those babies, and then dispatched the newborn by crushing its tiny skull with a rock. As a consequence of such rumor and gossip and in addition to everything else people could dream up, the Hill home became widely suspected of being a house of ill fame.

The female brigand was reportedly jailed a number of times by surrounding towns or counties. A military tribunal sentenced Nancy to hang for the shooting of a soldier at Fort Richardson. Storytellers assert that as guards dragged her from the courtroom she screamed, "I can break out of this old jail with a corset stay!" True or not, she evidently returned to Littleton's Springs a short time later and continued leading the gang in its thievery and mayhem.

At a time when a "decent" woman never rode astride a horse or visited saloons and drank like a man, Nancy Hill did both and laughed in the faces of those who might object. Talk flew thick and fast that she never passed up a chance to steal a horse or anything else that wasn't nailed down and usually traveled in the company of at least two or three hard-looking men who helped with her bold-as-brass crime sprees.

Physical descriptions paint the picture of an ordinary but not unattractive lady, inclined toward men's clothing and a brace of pistols. Those who freely offered food or help during surprise visits to rural homes even went so far as to say that Nancy could be downright friendly and generous in her payment for a meal. Charles Atchison, son of one of the original pioneer founders of Littleton's Springs, professed to have met the female outlaw while fetching water from a creek on the family's property. Mr. Atchison said that the mysterious woman asked if he'd ever heard of Nancy Hill. When he acknowledged that he had, the smiling horse thief lifted her skirts to reveal a pair of men's pants and "a hundred pistols." She then invited herself to his home for lunch, thanked the family for its kindness, and made the somewhat enigmatic statement, "I could never harm such kind people," as she spurred her horse away.

An apocryphal little gem, seemingly designed to make certain her reputation as a woman crazed by her own outlawry, involved the sadistic and brutal murder of a totally innocent pig. In an effort to demonstrate that she was the most evil member of the whole wicked crew, the story spread that "a man" (name conveniently unknown), disturbed by sounds of shots, screaming, cursing, and squealing animals coming from his sty, investigated to find a sight beyond belief. Mr. Name Unknown claimed that Nancy Hill wrestled in the slops with one of his wounded hogs. Her noted skill with a pistol appeared to have failed, and the stunned animal had recovered. The crazed woman, coated with blood, pig leavings, and whatever else you can imagine, laughed like a thing possessed as she finished the thrashing porker off with a knife. The storyteller, bereft of the necessary courage to put an end to such mischief and possessed of enough discretion to realize that his life could be lost over a hog, skulked away to tell his tale to neighbors over a beer down at Brazell's popular dram shop.

Brazell's Saloon became the favorite watering hole for Nancy's scruffy bunch, and it wasn't uncommon to see all six of the sisters swagger in wearing pistols and accompanied by a band of renegades that could number as high as twenty or more. On August 22, 1873, Nancy and a number of her criminal associates stormed Brazell's, tied the owner hand and foot, threw him onto the pool table, and proceeded to drink themselves silly while breaking up all his furniture and shooting off their guns at everything in general and nothing in particular.

Sometime during the day's festivities, a local big-talkin', little-doin' member of the bunch named Dave Porter stumbled into Tarkington's store and tried to walk off with a pair of new boots. Tom Tarkington stuck a double-barreled shotgun up the brazen thief's nose and politely told Porter he could have the boots when he could pay for them. Porter left but kept up a steady barrage of curses and threats as he made his exit.

By late afternoon the orgy of yelling, drinking, destruction, and gunfire had managed to rub each and every individual nerve in town raw. Just before it got dark, the whole crew of cutthroats mounted their horses, rode around the square shoutin', shootin', and generally scarin' the hell out of anyone on the street. Nancy, Porter, and another man, whose identity is unknown, broke away from their friends and rode their horses to the front of Tarkington's. The storekeeper and a boy named Johnny Laird were moving display merchandise off the boardwalk in preparation for that night's closing. The drunken trio of outlaws fired off a barrage that left Laird writhing in pain from a gunshot to the stomach. Stunned witnesses watched as the shooters wheeled their horses and fled. Whatever patience and forbearance the town's good people might have possessed for the Hills and their wild behavior ended that very minute on the boardwalk in front of Tarkington's.

Quicker'n a cat with its tail on fire, the entire town armed itself and stormed off in angry pursuit. But the outlaws proved elusive, and the hastily formed posse returned empty-handed. A freed slave, Sang Kirby—famed as a cowboy and Indian fighter—agreed to help track the killers. Late the following day, August 23, 1873, the vigilantes ran the murdering scum to ground in the dry bed of Denton Creek just across the Montague County line.

More than a little confusion exists in the second-, third-, and fourth-hand retellings of exactly what happened next. Nearly fifty years after the actual event, Tom Tarkington advised his niece—Mrs. Clyde Gear Beaty—that furious vigilantes spotted a stout tree limb, threw a noose over it, and led Nancy's horse into place. Porter and his friend were forced to their knees on either side of the animal. The angry woman, defiant to the end, had her horse whipped from beneath her, and the two men were summarily shot to death and left where they fell.

Shocking news of the lynching quickly spread all over the county and beyond. Rumors, thicker'n bunkhouse chili, abounded that threats made by the remaining Hill gang included clear-cut possibilities the entire town would be burned to the ground. Whatever the people of Littleton's Springs might have expected, the family of brigands again surprised everyone with the form of its retribution.

For some time the tiny community had anticipated becoming a regular stop on a local stage route between Fort Worth and Jacksboro. Dollar signs floated up in everyone's eyes as visions of potential prosperity in the form of new barns for the necessary animals, boarding facilities for hungry passengers, and, most importantly, an urgently needed link to the outside world approached.

The much-anticipated inauguratory run took place shortly after Nancy Hill assumed room temperature. The citizenry tried to put aside its fears and planned a party for the first coach's arrival. A few days before the big event, Johnny Laird finally died from his stomach wound, and although a spirit of confident expectation seemed to be in order, many in the crowd of celebrants feared what might take place on the most important day in the town's short history.

As the crowd waited, gunfire erupted on the roadway south of town a few minutes before the stage arrived—minus its driver and shotgun guard. Shouting and the sounds of numerous running animals were heard, and a large cloud of dust gave ample evidence that a party of riders was headed for refuge at the Hills' place. After discovery of the dead driver and his partner, another posse quickly formed and rushed directly to the bandit clan's farm. They found the crude house deserted but managed to overtake Martha and Katherine a short distance away in a spot known today as Hangman's Hollow. Everyone understood the drill. In less time than it would take for heaven's gate to slam in the face of a horse thief, Martha and Kate Hill were dancin' to the tune of that ol' fiddler death. Not satisfied with a double lynching, the company of vigilantes stormed back to the farm and reduced the Hills' rugged cabin to a pile of smoldering ashes.

If any organization or leadership of this second group of citizen justice-seekers existed, it vanished as their bloodlust built to an absolute fevered pitch while the pursuit proceeded apace. Somewhere near Agnes, a tiny community west of Littleton's Springs, the mob finally caught up with the remnants of Allen Hill's fractured family. Dusky Hill and her daughters Adeline and Eliza were shot to death. The two youngest children, Belle and Allen Jr., who were only eleven or twelve years old, respectively, were spared. They became wards of the town for a time and were eventually adopted by Sheriff Wes Hedrick of Parker County. Their individual fates are still open to speculation.

Those God-fearin', good folk who didn't necessarily approve of the lynchings, found themselves in a terrible quandary. They wanted to remove all the bodies for Christian burial but, because emotions still ran pretty hot, feared the possible consequences of such charitable actions. The dead women were left hanging from the trees or rotting where they fell for so long that Texas Rangers had to be called in to collect the remains. Most sources tend to agree that former Texas Ranger Captain Al Thompson, along with Rangers Doc Maupin and Montgomery Roe gathered up the decaying bodies of the Hill women. They buried the gruesome collection of hair, bones, and clothing inside a single large dry goods box in the town's cemetery and left the noose used on Nancy Hill dangling from a nearby tree as the dead women's only marker.

No definitive legal or newspaper account of the complete blood-soaked episode was ever recorded. However, on December 12, 1873, a Montague County Court approved payment for Constable William Slack's inquest over the body of one "Nancy Hill." The jury found that Nancy departed this life by being hanged by a person or persons unknown. The identities of the men who made up the posse remain a mystery to this day.

Some writers and observers have long harbored the opinion that these events were as much an outgrowth of the anger generated from the hatred locals harbored for "Yankee sympathizers," as any cattle and horse stealing the Hills might or might not have conducted. Lynching, as a method to rid a community of real or perceived problems, did not gain widespread acceptance until the lawlessness of the Civil War, and its aftermath left many communities of the South in a state of virtual anarchy. The most blatant example of such behavior in Texas took place during a two-week period in October of 1862. Called the Great Hanging at Gainsville, vigilantes dispatched over forty suspected Unionists as a result of tensions generated by the "unpleasantness."

Whatever the bottom line on Allen Hill and his family of high-spirited women might eventually become, it must be admitted that men with no criminal background; men considered leaders of the community; fine, upstanding citizens armed themselves and committed acts so violent and brutal as to border on the unbelievable. But believe we must. For although almost one hundred thirty years have passed since the events of those terrible few days, their names may have faded from memory, but their deeds are still with us.

# CHAPTER 11

———— •◦• ————

# AKA Carlotta J. Thompkins, Mystic Maude, and the Angel of San Antonio

## Lottie Deno

The convoluted pathways women took to Texas after the Civil War proved as varied as those of the men they usually followed. Carlotta J. Thompkins is believed to have started life amidst the bluegrass and blue bloods of Warsaw, Kentucky, on April 21, 1844. Like most of the wealthy residents of that state, the Thompkins family loved a good horse race, and the beautiful Lottie's father raised thoroughbred animals primarily for that single purpose. Breeders and handlers, from far and wide, knew the handsome gambler was more than willing to throw down a bet or turn a card at the drop of a horse fritter.

At some point before the Great Fight for Southern Independence, Thompkins, accompanied by his daughter, made a raid on the continent. The legend follows that young Lottie acquired her skill at poker and other games of chance as a result of their frequent and entertaining visits to the most popular European casinos of the day. Shortly after their return to the states, Fort Sumter fell. Fighting and death swept the entire country full-bore. Early in the fracas her father was killed, and the aristocratic family's standing and fortunes eventually went the way of the Confederacy.

Lottie's mother and younger, more homely sister found themselves with a sizable plantation to run and little in the way of funds. In an effort to save themselves and their southern pride, lovely Lottie got shipped off to Detroit at age eighteen with instructions to find a suitable husband. Suitable, meaning one with the proper social status. Why a southern belle got sent off to Detroit, of all places, to find a spouse is beyond me, but hey, mythology is what it is.

At any rate, Lottie, chaperoned by a seven-foot-tall black nanny named Mary Poindexter, hit Detroit looking for a bridegroom. But, lo and behold, fate stepped up and threw a kink in the plan when she bumped into one of her father's former jockeys, a quick-talking, good-looking, silver-tongued devil named Johnny Golden. (If this doesn't sound like a dime novel romance, I'll eat the felt off a poker table.) Johnny evidently had some prior knowledge of Lottie's skill with a deck of cards and per-suaded her to sit in on some of his games.

Quicker'n a Baptist deacon takin' up Sunday collections, Lottie and her handsome rogue were making money hand over fist. Just about a heartbeat-and-a-half after that, they were doing so well he lured her into an assault on riverboat gamblers who traveled the Ohio and Mississippi. The girl's remaining family had a fit of the collective vapors and dis-owned her for being a good Christian who had cast her religious teach-ings aside and associated herself with, God save her, a man of the Jewish persuasion. If such parental disapproval had any effect, you couldn't tell it from appearances. Lottie, in the company of her gigantic nanny, and Johnny Golden traveled the rivers during some of the worst years of the "unpleasantness," but parted company in late 1863. They planned a reunion in San Antonio, but that ol' devil fate stepped in again. Mary Poindexter and her precocious ward landed in New Orleans for a spell and did eventually end up in San Antonio in 1865. Unfortunately, the fast talkin' Johnny didn't show his good-lookin', deceitful face until almost five years later.

While she waited for her lovin' man's return, Lottie sharpened her skills at the tables by working as a house gambler for the Thurmonds, a Georgia family who owned a joint called the University Club. In no time at all she was wallowin' in velvet and had fallen head over stacked poker deck in love with Frank Thurmond, gamblin' son of the University Club's southern-fried owners. She became so popular and well known, locals affectionately called her the "Angel of San Antonio."

Sometime in 1869 Johnny popped in on the cooing turtle doves and told everyone within shouting distance that Lottie Thompkins was his wife. Lottie hotly denied any such matrimonial connection to Golden. The entire three-way love situation became considerably more complicated when Frank Thurmond got into a shootin' match with a double-dealing fellow who made the mistake of a-reachin' and a-fumblin'. Thurmond put several large holes in the man and split for the wilder parts of North Texas when pressure from local law enforcement types got too hot to handle. Lottie immediately packed her bags and set out to find him. She gambled from one frontier town to another—Fort Concho (where she took the sobriquet *Mystic Maude*), Jacksboro, San Angelo, Denison, and Fort Worth—before finally settling at Fort Griffin.

The dust from Lottie's departure of San Antonio had barely settled when Johnny Golden got involved in a little ol' corpse and cartridge affair of his own. He snuffed another fellow's candle and ended up ridin' the outlaw trail himself.

Lottie's entrance on the Fort Griffin scene caused quite a stir. She arrived in 1876 on the Jacksboro stage, sitting up-top with driver Dick Wheeler. Beautiful women in such a place were a rarity, and those who would ride on top of the coach virtually nonexistent. From that moment until her eventual departure, she separated herself from the rest of the violent and fluid population of the area by taking a shanty near the Clear Fork of the Brazos and leaving it only to visit local mercantile stores and work as a professional card dealer in the Bee Hive Saloon's gambling room.

Fort Griffin and the bustling village below it, called the "Bottom" or the "Flat," was as wild and woolly as any western town of dubious reputation that ever existed. It was a community where all the hoot-owls sang bass and, while growing at the foot of Government Hill, soon filled with rogues, gamblers, bullwhackers, gunhawks, and prostitutes whose only mission in life was to fleece the unsuspecting and practice their ungodly trades.

Living conditions for the enlisted soldiers of Fort Griffin bordered on the crudest, most spartan level imaginable. As a consequence, the men frequently rioted, drunken corruption was commonplace, fistfights, gunfights, knife fights, and worse were daily events. Hospital personnel treated numerous patients for injuries sustained when fighting erupted between Negro and white soldiers, or between Negro soldiers and civilians. The worst wounds during these semi-friendly dustups were usually inflicted with a double-bit axe.

Assistant Surgeon D. G. Caldwell filed reports making it quite clear that most of the problems he faced were caused by whiskey supplied by local sutlers. Abominable weather conditions compounded all existing difficulties. In one instance, in July 1870, almost seven inches of rain fell in less than five hours forcing Collins Creek and the Clear Fork of the Brazos out of their banks and into the shacks and shanties of the Flat. Three years later Caldwell reported that troopers had been excused from all their drill ... "because of a severe dust storm."

The streets stayed congested day and night with horses, wagons, hacks, and buggies. In an effort to attract drunks to their watering holes, saloon owners hired fiddle, banjo, and guitar players who sang at the top of their lungs while scantily dressed whores pranced up and down the boardwalks in an effort to add to the seductive allure of such places.

Between 1875 and 1880, the rowdy population of the tenuous town almost doubled. It grew into a village of over a thousand permanent residents and at least that many temporary types, including buffalo hunters, cowboys, and those who just tended to generally move west when civilization caught up with them.

The Flat's ungodly and dangerous lifestyle provided plenty of copy for the *Frontier Echo* of Jacksboro. In one issue they published the following: "Cowboys raising hell in town last night. Marshall William C. Gilson put a load of buckshot in the chest and arm of William Harpe, though he was not seriously hurt." Kinda makes you wonder just what it would have taken to inflict something like serious injury on a man of Mr. Harpe's type.

Lottie Thompkins rode into this mass of seething lawlessness and depravity like a fairy princess atop her magic pumpkin. Shortly after her arrival, she took to calling herself Lottie Deno. This alias was thought to be the result of a fellow cardplayer referring to her as "Lotta Dinero" because of her unerring ability to separate the stupid bumpkin from his money. Gamblers who walked away from the southern lady's table shaking their heads at her proficiency included the likes of Doc Holliday, Wyatt Earp, and other well-known figures of western legend and myth.

Holliday supposedly played a major part in the single instance of Lottie publicly losing her head and going for a gun. Seems Big Nose Kate, a woman notorious for her depraved conduct, accused Lottie of trying to steal Doc away from her. At least Lottie had the nerve to point out the man's shortcomings. "Why, you low-down slinking slut. If I should step in soft cow manure, I would not clean my foot on that bastard!" Can't get much clearer than that. 'Course there is some question as to whether this event ever actually took place. Given Carlotta Thompkins's upbringing, it does tend to sound like her. I don't know about anyone else, but I think I'll believe it—every word.

Lottie's amazing ability to keep her head around the likes of Holliday, Big Nose Kate, and others of even worse ilk, manifested itself the night a pistol fight broke out at her table. Several hard cases got to yelling charges of cold deckin', marked cards, and seconds dealin' at one another. Smoky Joe, Monte Bill, and an Arizona gambler went for their hand cannons and got to pitchin' lead back and forth across the table. As most of the all-gurgle-and-no-guts crowd trampled each other to get out the nearest door or window, Lottie simply pushed away from the table and moved to a safer corner. When Sheriff Jim Draper arrived, he inquired as to why she didn't run like everyone else. She pointed out that it happened too fast, and, besides, the corner was safe enough from the likes of this particular poor-shooting bunch. In her opinion, they had only managed to hit one another because of the quantity of lead pumped out.

Rumors, tall tales, and completely unfounded piles of horsefeathers about her identity followed Lottie every time she walked from her little shack to the Bee Hive. Some actually felt she lived the double life of a lady of means back East and desperate woman of the world in the West. Others had it on absolutely unimpeachable authority that the mysterious female gambler was a New Orleans philanthropist traveling incognito, and a third group clung to something along the lines of her actual background. No matter. She kept to herself at Fort Griffin—solitary to the point of being considered a recluse by all those who whispered their favorite fiction about her past.

Whatever the gamblers, whores, cardsharps, and others of their kind might have believed about her history, one thing they all felt for certain—she was a kept woman. Most believed Mike Fogerty, owner of the Bee Hive, did the keeping. Shucks and wazoo, guess what Mike Fogerty's real name turned out to be—that's right cowpokes and cowgals, lovin' man on the run, Frank Thurmond.

In the spring of 1877 none other than Johnny Golden reappeared. The man had an amazing capacity for showing up at the worst possible times. Since keeping his mouth shut wasn't one of Johnny's better developed skills, he quickly let it be known that he and Lottie Deno had been and were still married. Well, he picked the wrong place to play that sorry hand again.

A few nights after his wind-bellied, flannel-mouthed arrival, deputy sheriff Jim Draper and city marshal Bill Gilson found Golden at one of the Bee Hive's poker tables and accused him of stealing a horse. Gamblers, drunks, and general layabouts who witnessed the ensuing scuffle swore later that Golden had heatedly denied the charge as a scurrilous lie. Some even went so far as to say Golden loudly proclaimed that he had never even so much as owned a horse in his entire life. Didn't matter, Draper and Gilson muscled the protesting gambler into the dusty, unlit street and headed in the general, stumbling direction of Fort Griffin's military guardhouse. More than one of the witnesses scratched their heads and thought this somewhat odd since the local hoosegow was only about a hundred feet away at the opposite end of the street.

Next morning someone discovered Golden's bullet-riddled body behind Smith's wagon yard. Draper and Gilson first claimed a group of enraged citizens took their prisoner and killed him. When that windy whizzer didn't fly, they changed their story and declared that the gambler tried to run, and they were each forced to shoot the unarmed man several times in order to foil the thievin' bastard's attempted escape. Only problem with that particular story developed when the undertaker picked the body up and noticed that bullets had gone through the skinny outlaw and into the ground beneath him. One of the brighter members of the milling crowd suggested that the poor goober must have been lying on his back when he got seriously confronted with deadly gunfire.

A local justice of the peace hastily convened a hearing/inquest into the dubious demise of Johnny Golden. Quicker'n grasshoppers in a chicken yard, the killers were absolved of any culpability. About a minute after the final gavel fell, rumors started flying thick and fast that an enraged Fogerty/Thurmond (or an irate bartender named Shaunessey, take your pick) had paid the lawmen to leave Golden with more holes in him than a cabbage leaf after a hailstorm. The price set for the deadly disposal was $250.

A connected story has it that Johnny's father made the arduous journey from Illinois to Texas in the hope of finding out the truth of his son's unfortunate death. Upon his arrival in Fort Worth, the elder Mr. Golden got a cool reception, and blood-soaked threats were made on his life. The unnerved tenderfoot made a hasty exit with nothing in the way of the additional facts he'd hoped for.

Legend is that Lottie paid the $65 for Johnny Golden's funeral but couldn't bring herself to attend the services. She and Frank wisely parted company during the aftermath of the killing. They both hopped out of town quicker'n a herd of tree frogs. Rumor had it that she left the Flat with $20,000 in poker winnings packed inside a small leather trunk.

Soon as the dust settled from her stage departure, locals expressed a desire to see what she'd left in her little shack, but since her rent was paid up for another month, no one had nerve enough to go inside. When the sheriff returned from out of town, he broke the lock on Lottie's private world. Her tiny room was decorated floor to ceiling with the finest of everything money could buy. A note, pinned to the pillow of her bed, admonished the finder to sell it all and give the money to those in need.

For a time Lottie lived alone in Jacksboro but joined forces with Thurmond again in Kingston, New Mexico, where they ran a small game in a backroom at the Victoria Hotel. On December 2, 1880, the couple finally married in Silver City, New Mexico. She signed the certificate as Carlotta J. Thompkins, which is thought to be her real name.

From the time of their marriage, Frank and Lottie Thurmond lived in Deming, New Mexico, where they operated a restaurant. At some point Frank tried his hand at mining, then real estate, and eventually banking at Deming National, where he became a highly respected vice president. J. Marvin Hunter claimed to have known Lottie during the Deming period. He described her as sweet natured and gracious to a fault, but noted that all their friends warned against ever getting into any kind of card game with Lottie or her husband.

After Frank's death, Lottie dedicated the rest of her life to charity work conducted by the St. Luke's Episcopal Church. With her passing on February 9, 1934, and burial beside her beloved husband, stories surfaced purporting to be the last word on her checkered past. She and Frank became models for characters in a series of books written by Alfred Henry Lewis, and Miss Kitty of television's *Gunsmoke* fame owed everything about her characterization to the legend of Lottie Deno, as did Laura Denbo in the 1957 western *Gunfight at the OK Corral.*

Within months of her departure from the Flat, the army closed Fort Griffin. The soldiers, buffalo hunters, cowboys, pimps, whores, gamblers, and grifters vanished like a cloud of gunsmoke drifting away from Lottie's table at the Bee Hive. The army had killed off the Comanches in the Palo Duro, and the days of the great cattle drives had ended forever. In less time that it would take an old maid to crawl under a bed, Fort Griffin and the Flat were nothing more than dust, third-hand stories, and memories.

# CHAPTER 12

―•●•―

# NEKKID, NEKKID, NEKKID!
## Adah Isaacs Menken

J ust about a week before work on this chapter started, a sometime
singer, actress, and personality of our day appeared on an internationally televised awards program in as close to a state of undress as you
can get and still be allowed in public. Her barely clothed body proved
an old adage that has governed the conscious thoughts of every other
male on the planet since the beginning of time—there's just nothing like
a partially, or better yet, completely nekkid woman to get our undivided
attention.

The overly endowed young lady, who proudly and repeatedly jiggled
her way across every newscast in the United States for three nights in a
row, isn't the first woman to realize this. Although—given our modern
media's response to the vast expanses of her ample bosom on display for
the world's prurient viewing—you would have thought so.

In point of actual fact, the paradigm for such behavior on the part of
American women might well have been a Nacogdoches, Texas beauty
who went, variously, by the names Ada Bertha Theodore, Adelaide
McCord, Ada C. McCord, Dolores Adios, Marie Rachel Adelaide de
Vere Spenser, and, most often, Adah Isaacs Menken. Born June 15,
1835, in Memphis, Tennessee, Ms. Menken's life prior to her achievement of cosmopolitan notability is hazy at best, downright obscure and

sometimes goofy at worst, and decidedly vague virtually all the rest of the time.

The confusion about her origins—and nearly every other fact surrounding her early private life—which followed her during her entire career and in virtually every corner of the world she visited, could easily be laid directly at the dainty feet of Ms. Menken herself. When asked by newspaper reporters of her day where she entered this world, her birthplace shifted from New Orleans, Milneburg, or Chartrain, Louisiana, to Nacogdoches, Texas, or Memphis, Tennessee, and even parts of Spain, depending on the phase of the moon and whether her makeup looked the way she wanted it that day. Ethnic derivations tap-danced from Creole to French, Scotch-Irish, Spanish, Jewish, and even African American. A similar lack of definitive information about her family included references to a stepfather whose name got bandied around as Campbell, Josephs, or McCord. Seems that if the lovely Adah hadn't gone into showbiz, she'd have made a top-notch politician.

The only thing we know for sure about that early period of the truth-bending lady's existence is that she spent *some time* in Nacogdoches and *claimed* to have attended the local university. Court documents, legal filings, and census records shed no light at all on this chapter of her life. Families named Campbell and McCord did live in the area at that point, and the Campbells did have several daughters. But no record that can be matched to Ms. Menken has yet turned up. Another anecdote insists that supposed father or stepfather McCord or Campbell ran a mercantile store near the site of Nacogdoches's Old Stone Fort. The myth has the sound of another of Adah's rambling and deceptive explanations concerning her early life.

At a time and place still shrouded in the great unknown, she began what would eventually become her career in theater. Professional theater had started slowly in Texas, centered itself in the more densely populated areas along the coast, and attracted audiences that tended to be comprised of rowdy frontiersmen who drank, fought, and fired off their pistols during performances. The law-abiding citizens, where these groups sprang up, often questioned the necessity and morality of such offerings and openly compared those who practiced the acting vocation to pimps and prostitutes. Those high-toned folk probably had some legitimate gripes, because the presentations from traveling players could range from serious stage performances and musical offerings to a hodge-podge of the most scandalous diversions imaginable.

Adah and her less attractive sister, Josephine—acting as a chaper-one—might have started touring these coastal centers of culture as early as 1850. Both are said to have entertained in Galveston that year, and sto-ries exist that credit the beautiful Adah—wearing a set of shocking pink tights—with having rendered a high-wire act that reportedly stunned, delighted, and mesmerized audiences. She later claimed to have learned the wire-walking trick and her skill on horseback when she started her acting career as a twelve-year-old performer in New Orleans or maybe while traveling around the countryside with a circus.

The most bizarre tale of how she achieved amazingly proficient equine skills makes the extravagant assertion that at some point in the 1850s wild Indians captured her while she hunted buffalo near Port Lavaca. But Lord be praised, a band of Texas Rangers under the command of Frederick Harney charged in and rescued the vivacious twenty-year-old beauty. Ranger Harney was so taken with the young enchantress he immediately adopted her and hired tutors to teach the stunning young goddess the arts of sculpture and painting. Adah promptly repaid that courageous, formidable, and benevolent gentle-man's generosity by falling madly, passionately, and, presumably, physi-cally in love with her instructor. Harney did exactly what you would have expected any kind, benevolent, loving *man* to do—he kicked her sorry behind out into the wilds of Indian-infested Texas to make it on her own.

People who liked that cloud of corral dust just loved the other version of the same tale where Adah's savior was none other than Sam Houston himself. But according to that rendition, she quickly grew tired of Houston's house full of noisy, difficult, bratty kids, ran away, and joined a Mexico-bound ballet troupe. One biographer even has her Native American captor described as an Apache brave who renounced his Apacheness for love of Adah, and the length of her captivity varies in these yarns from three weeks to several years. Some of them include the noble Indian chief Eagle Eye. It is claimed that Mr. Eye taught Adah to ride like a Comanche, shoot like Buffalo Bill, and even toughened her up for any eventuality in the future.

Whatever actually happened—if anything really did—and whoever in fact saved her from a fate worse than death—all of which is highly questionable—it seems that even at this early stage of her life, Adah Bertha Theodore had a talent for manipulating the facts surrounding anyone and anything she ever came into contact with.

In 1855 it's fairly certain the aspiring artiste and shapely beauty landed in Liberty, Texas, where she became friends with local newspaper editor Henry Shea and other prominent men in the community. Naturally, they just loved her performances and encouraged her to write poetry. A *Liberty Gazette* advertisement, dated October 8 of the same year, announced that public readings from Shakespeare would be conducted by Miss Ada Bertha Theodore. Poems and essays attributed to her appeared in later editions of the *Gazette* with datelines of Austin and Washington, Texas.

But, during this early period, her greatest ambition seemed to have been a desire to achieve some fame as a dramatic actress. Unfortunately, during a Nashville, Texas, Shakespearean offering for a fairly discriminating audience, she stumbled, mumbled, and bumbled her way through a rendition of Lady Macbeth. Adah rewrote so much of the bard that night that in one fell swoop she managed to start and end any career she might have coveted along those lines. From that point on she tended to restrict her efforts on stage to the melodramatic and sometimes played male roles.

Even offstage Adah adopted that period's well-defined affectations of the tragic heroine. She projected a mysterious sadness that seemingly never left her. She rarely smiled and often sighed heavily while in the company of others—especially the more easily fooled members of the species, men. She claimed no women as friends and never spoke of any incidents in her past that might have explained such behavior. The poor demented males, taken in by her obvious beauty and every man's ego-driven mantra that "there's always a chance," speculated endlessly about the sorrowful and unfortunate background that could cause such despondency in the mysterious and beautiful young actress and poet.

In April 1856 she delivered something of a heavy-duty blow to all the "there's always a chance" crowd and married a Jewish theatrical musician named Alexander Isaacs Menken. Menken's major claim to fame is his place in history as the first of Adah's several husbands—legal and otherwise. After the limited and questionable success of her theater engagements along the coast—and upon her insistence—the couple moved to Cincinnati to be near her new husband's family. While there, she accepted Judaism as her faith and claimed at various times throughout the rest of her life to have been born Jewish.

But a year's worth of washing, cooking, scrubbing, and general domestic-goddess-type stuff appears to have been just about as much as a woman with footlights in her eyes, like Adah, could take. Her husband no longer felt the siren call of sawdust, applause, and makeup, and the pair went their separate ways on the strength of a rabbinical diploma that supposedly dissolved their hasty and ill-fated marriage.

In 1857 she sprinted back to Shreveport, Louisiana, and debuted as Pauline in *The Lady of Lyons,* moved on to New Orleans and acted as Bianca in *Fazio,* and in March 1859 scrambled to New York and dazzled audiences with her beauty as the Widow Cheerly in *The Soldier's Daughter.*

While playing in New York, she met, married, and became pregnant by John C. Heenan, a well-known Irish prizefighter. Before the child's birth, former hubby Menken popped up again, called on every yellow journalist in town, and proclaimed loudly to all who would listen that he and the lovely Adah were still husband and wife. The scandal fell right into the middle of her new relationship like a dead juggler dropped from one of the stage flats. Rather than wait for an explanation, the sensitive and thoughtful Heenan promptly abandoned the pregnant Adah. The pair was eventually divorced after Heenan's son died in infancy. Like some of Sally Skull's husbands, Menken simply disappeared from the scene.

Once the Civil War got underway, jobs for actresses got harder to find than bluebonnets in October. Adah kept herself in tortillas and lip rouge by writing and reading her own poetry in coffeehouses and got herself published often enough in Hebrew books, magazines, and newspapers to become fairly well known. Then, in June 1861, opportunity finally came a knocking at her stage door, and Adah grabbed him by the collar, threw him to the floor, and pinned him for the count.

At Albany's Green Street Theater, she began a starring run in *Mazeppa; or The Wild Horse of Tartary,* a melodrama based on one of George Gordon, Lord Byron's poems. Quicker'n a Texas blue norther a rippin' through Manhattan, Adah Isaacs Menken became an overnight sensation the likes of which even jaded New Yorkers had never seen.

During a stunningly staged scene of thunder, lightning, and blowing snow, that feisty Texas gal strapped herself to the back of a horse and rode onto stage. This was nothing out of the ordinary. Other women had done as much before in the same play, but they all appeared wearing a brightly colored Tartar costume. Not our sweet little ol' Adah. She brought a whole new interpretation to the role. Through a combination

*"The Naked Lady"—Adah Isaacs Menken. Not quite naked, as pictured here, but the photo easily conveys the beauty men on two continents found completely irresistible.* Courtesy Theatre Arts Collection Harry Ransom Humanities Research Center-University of Texas at Austin

of careful lighting, a flesh-toned set of skin-hugging silk tights, and a carefully draped piece of diaphanous cloth, Adah Isaacs Menken appeared to be totally, absolutely, and beyond any shadow of a doubt nekkid, nekkid, nekkid. Women in the audience gasped and fluttered behind their fans. Red-faced men sweated lakes into their high-priced seats while thoughts of how they could get backstage after the performance raced through their fevered brains. The squirming response of the audiences caused by the impact of her seemingly unclothed body is especially commanding when you consider that she played the part of *Prince* Mazeppa.

In that single audacious moment on the night of June 3, 1861, the seemingly bare-bottomed Adah took Albany and the rest of New York by storm. The next day she was celebrated in newspapers all over America and the Continent as "The Naked Lady." Theater owners in all the capitals of Europe clamored for presentation of her flamboyant performance for their more discriminating and appreciative audiences. Overnight

"The Naked Lady" became the highest paid actress in the world. For the next several years the curtain on her melodramatic offering went up in virtually every city in the Northeast, Midwest, parts of the West, San Francisco, and eventually to overwhelming response in Europe.

Leaders of the Northern oppressors during the War of Yankee Aggression would like to believe that the impact of her seemingly naked body was such that on June 14, 1861, nine of the Union army's finest generalissimos attended her opening in New York City and left the theater in such a state of individual male flusterationism that their befuddlement caused them to go out and lose the First Battle of Bull Run the following month. If such a fantasy came anywhere close to being true, Robert E. Lee would most likely have seen to it that "The Naked Lady" did her show for every Union general opposing him at least twice a week.

Some critics of the time referred to Adah as the "most undressed female performer now on the American stage." Mark Twain, who caught her act in Virginia City, Nevada, called the lovely Adah little more than a "shape artist" starring in a "leg show." Considering her costume it's pretty clear what he meant. But Twain also let it be known her "leg show" was worth every cent of admission and conceded that even if Adah's talent didn't extend much past extra fine female limbs and a stunning bust, he had to admit she was a damned fine shape artist. Nevada City miners agreed wholeheartedly and turned out in grubby droves to shout encouragement as Prince Mazeppa tore through the imaginary Polish countryside of staged fantasies clothed in not so much as a "shirt collar or pair of spurs."

In 1864 "The Naked Lady" took her show to London and Paris. By that time she had married and divorced another husband, Robert Henry Newell, a Civil War satirist who wrote using the pen name Orpheus C. Kerr—which meant "office seeker." They took the vows in 1862 and divorced three years later.

In Europe, newspapers often linked her name to steamy relationships with French writer Alexandre Dumas, pére, and English poet Algernon Charles Swinburne. The sanctimonious Swinburne later denied any such *affaire de amour* in the best red-faced English style, but no one believed him. And at some point, between performances of *Mazeppa* and her numerous intrigues, she also found the wherewithal to get married again in 1866 to a gambler named James Paul Barclay. Barclay presented her with a second child. The notorious George Sand acted as godmother to the baby, whom Adah named Louis Dudevant Victor Emmanuel. Some say Louis also died in infancy, others that his whereabouts are simply unknown.

Descendants of a gentleman named William Henry Harrison Davenport claimed that he was married to Adah at some point during all this *Sturm und Drang,* but when ol' William Henry found out about her romantic intrigue with novelist Dumas, the supposedly rejected and dejected hubby took a hike for the Australian outback and the company of kangaroos. There might have been other affairs—and husbands. Some writers believe Adah said "I do" as often as six and maybe even seven times, while conducting so many outrageous, scandalous, and sordid liaisons that a circus ringmaster couldn't have kept track of all of them. Truth is Adah never seemed all that concerned about marriage certificates, divorce decrees, and other such trivial matters. She even went so far as to get married at least twice before legal papers dissolving a current marriage could be finalized on the most recently dumped spouse.

Her public persona might have looked like a hormone-driven mess, but she peopled her private life with some of the most famous writers of the day. From her earliest ventures into the arts, Adah had always considered herself a poet. The fame and wealth *Mazeppa* brought made it possible to spend a goodly amount of whatever spare time she had with well-known men of letters like Twain, Bret Harte, Walt Whitman, Dante Gabriel Rossetti, and Charles Dickens. Dickens is believed to have acted as editor of a volume of Adah's poetry published in 1868 titled *Infelicia,* and she even went so far as to dedicate one of her other collections of verses to him.

Though some of her writing wasn't bad, critics of her day didn't care much for it, and there were some who even claimed she hired others to produce it for her. The most stinging commentaries centered on her confusing and emotional passages that tended to be devoted to an endless amount of self-centered navel-gazing.

A Galveston newspaper turned out to be one of Adah's most bitter faultfinders. Editors and staff writers had little good to say about the celebrated actress and world's most photographed woman. *Blake's Semi-Weekly Galveston Bulletin* never missed a chance to point out her shortcomings as a writer or performer and openly criticized her bohemian attitudes toward marriage and children. The paper punished her repeatedly for seemingly using her divorces as a means of attracting public attention and administered a number of word-lashings for giving birth to several children, which were immediately forgotten when the newest male flame in the bonfire of her life managed to leap forward—and, of course, one always did.

In spite of such sordid charges, Ms. Menken was considered kindhearted to the extreme, the ultimate soft-touch by many, and ended up suffering terribly because of it. Theater owners around the world made her one of the world's richest women, but she squandered it all on an extravagant lifestyle of parties, clothing, and the gambling debts of two former husbands. A lifelong concern for young thespians less fortunate than herself made her an easy target for any would-be actors with their hands out. She threw money at all those she considered downtrodden and donated heavily to virtually every charity bold enough to request a contribution.

In the winter of 1867, with her career in America locked in steep decline, her financial problems became so pronounced that she returned to England and performed briefly in a new production of *Mazeppa.*

Unfortunately, a jaded public, who had been there and seen that, preferred a rival presentation of the same show and stayed away by the thousands. Any hopes she harbored of a revived career and fat new bank account were dashed by box office receipts so poor she abruptly abandoned the project and fled to Paris.

In the spring of 1868 Adah agreed to a Parisian revival of one of her other favorite old standbys, a buckle and swash epic called *Les Pirates de la Savanne.* On August 10, scheduled as opening day for rehearsals, the company's theater manager found the world's most famous "Naked Lady" dead at her dressing table. She was only thirty-three years old. Her mysterious passing caused almost as much talk, and the flow of as much printers ink, as had her tumultuous life. Suspicious writers at *Blake's Semi-Weekly Galveston Bulletin* professed absolute disbelief of her reported fate and even went so far as to charge her with nothing more than another effort at shameless self-promotion. No definitive reason for her demise ever surfaced. Some said her health had been in decline for months, and others that complications from an unidentified injury inflicted while she performed in London were responsible. As has been observed previously, it was incredibly easy to die a hundred fifty years ago. Powerful women like Sarah Bowman were proof that something as simple as an insect bite could put you in the ground. Rumors exist that she died alone or in the presence of a faithful maid and cruel theater manager who had called the gendarmes on her for failing to appear ready for his rehearsal. And still another version of the scene declares that, ever true to her adopted religious beliefs, God tore her ticket for that big theater in the sky with a rabbi in attendance.

Adah Isaacs Menken's body was buried in Paris's Cimetiere Du Pere Lachaise. For those who've never visited Pere Lachaise, it is enough you know that for a while she rested among some of the most revered writers, politicians, and figures of fame in the history of France up until that time. Eternally sleeping in the company of the likes of Honore de Balzac,

Marie-Joseph Chernier, and Jean-Baptiste Moliere had to have been of some otherworldly spiritual comfort for the deeply religious Adah. Later, her remains were disinterred and moved to the Jewish section of the Cimetere Du Montparnasse, a short distance south of Le Jardin Du Luxembourg. A single, monolithic stone over the grave notes her name, place of birth, and date of death. On one side of the stone—prominently decorated with an urn—is the cryptic message, "Thou knowest."

But her story doesn't end at Montparnasse. A woman of Adah's power and impact often influences the lives of others for years after she is no longer counted among the living. Such was the case with "The Naked Lady." In 1902, thirty-four years after her death, the editor of the *Houston Daily Telegraph*, Tom Ochiltree, also passed away. Shortly after his demise an article appeared in the *St. Louis Globe-Democrat* titled "The Christmas Present Santa Brought to Tom Ochiltree."

In a touching recollection of his early years as a Texas Ranger, the old newspaperman described the torch he had carried a lifetime for the unforgettably beautiful teenager he knew as Adah Bertha Theodore. The Adah of his childhood dreams still lived in a log cabin on the edge of the wilderness with her unassuming father and stunningly beautiful, well-educated mother.

After years of secret adolescent longing for Adah, a young Tom Ochiltree returned to Nacogdoches unscathed by his first encounter with Comanche Indians and accepted an invitation to be present at a Christmas-eve party attended by fellow Rangers and friends from the surrounding countryside. Amid all the dancing and merriment Adah supposedly sat enthralled as Tom's friends described his gallantry and courage in the heat of battle.

As the party progressed, a heavy-duty rainstorm settled in, and the revelers decided to stay over for the night. In an effort to maintain the gala mood and continue to celebrate the coming of Christmas, everyone began hanging up his or her socks or stockings. Adah batted her biggest girly eyes at the shy female-intimidated Ochiltree and urged him to make sure he put up a stocking. She implied that there just wasn't much telling what he might get. But poor Ochiltree felt he had an unsolvable problem. He had danced all evening with such abandon and vigor that his toes had punched huge holes in his pitiful socks. In desperation, and urged on by more eye batting and insinuation from Adah, he decided to hang his boots instead.

The next morning the boots had disappeared, and as others sampled the candies and sweet treats found in their stockings, poor Tom tried to put on a manly face by accepting the assessment of a friend who suggested that, "Mexicans must have stolen them." As the morning progressed someone provided him with a pair of slippers. At breakfast Adah seemed to avoid him, and although he tried to maintain his manly exterior, it cut poor Tom to the quick when she avoided his best flirtatious glances. That is until she later stepped out in the crowd wearing his boots.

Ochiltree lovingly carried the memory of what Santa left in his boots to the grave. For a single moment in the drabness and uncertainty of frontier life a beautiful girl did something he never forgot. Evidently nothing else in his existence came close in comparison. Not an adventurous life as a Texas Ranger, status as a Confederate war hero, politician, well-known journalist, or world traveler. Any man who hasn't had the same feelings for an unapproachable woman at some point in his life hasn't really lived. Tom Ochiltree counted himself a lucky man because he knew Adah Isaacs Menken. How could he have felt otherwise?

# CHAPTER 13

———•◦•———

# A Good Girl Gone Bad
## Bonnie Parker

Any book touting itself as informing the tender reader about the most notorious women of Texas that didn't include a chapter on Bonnie Parker wouldn't be worth the ink it would take to print it. No other American woman of infamous reputation has managed to inspire such a devoted and knowledgeable following as the tiny Dallas waitress who burst onto America's consciousness during the worst years of this country's Great Depression. Her's might well be the modern paradigm for the age-old story of the good girl gone bad.

The Lone Star State's most famous female outlaw of the twentieth century came into this world on October 1, 1910, in the West Texas town of Rowena (near San Angelo). Her father, Henry Parker, unexpectedly died before his daughter's fifth birthday. The family immediately migrated more than two hundred miles to an area of Dallas, then affectionately known as "Cement City," in order to take advantage of the support offered by remaining relatives.

Testimonials from teachers, principals, and local religious leaders glow with their praise of little Bonnie. Her childhood was about as normal as that of any other young girl who grew up at the time. No doubt she loved her dolly, skipped rope, played house, hopscotch, hide-and-seek, and probably beat the boys at dodge ball. She did extremely well at school and was reputed to harbor a love of the theatrical that resulted in private speech and drama lessons at an early age. Her scholastic skill hit its pinnacle when she won a citywide spelling contest as a student at Bryan High School.

Bonnie's popularity with those of the manly persuasion started at an early age. She never wanted for boyfriends, and male classmates showered her with gifts, candy, and constant attention. Even local politicians fell under the beautiful, red-haired girl's spell. Several county politicos, who felt that her dainty good looks drew favorable attention, showed her off at public rallies in much the same way campaign managers use movie stars today. The tiny girl didn't look or act the part of a soon-to-be-celebrated murderess, kidnapper, and thief.

In 1926, of all the men or boys she could have picked, Bonnie married one of her childhood sweethearts, a part-time thug and thief named Roy Thornton. Her hasty wedding might well have been the impetus for the destructive behavior that followed. Thornton easily fit the part of model for all her future associations with men. Their relationship has often been described as tumultuous at best and most likely abusive. Although the stormy marriage ended with his departure for a lengthy term in prison, she steadfastly refused to file for divorce even when friends and family pressured her to do so.

In 1929, at about the same time Thornton moved into the hoosegow, Marco's Cafe in Dallas closed, and nineteen-year-old Bonnie lost her job. Her sprite-like good looks and friendly manner made it easy to find other employment, and she quickly took a position waiting tables at the American Cafe on Houston Street.

The restaurant, located near the Dallas County Courthouse, enjoyed a good business because of its proximity to the downtown business district. Clerks, salesmen, secretaries, lawmen, and courthouse employees patronized the cafe. Bonnie's brassy good looks and flirtatious manner made her popular enough with male customers to keep a steady flow of tips coming her way in the darkest days of the Depression years.

In 1930 that indefinable, soul-killing lightning of human passion struck when a two-bit car thief and stickup artist named Clyde Barrow ordered a cup of coffee from Ms. Parker and forever changed her life. The sparks that flew between them sealed her eventual fate, and within a month of their star-crossed meeting, Clyde botched a burglary in Waco, and some pesky law types threw his worthless butt in jail. There's just no other way to look at it—some girls naturally like bad boys. (See chapter 9.)

Clyde had competition from another American Cafe patron named Ted Hinton, who would later claim a pivotal role in Bonnie's death. Hinton worked for the postal service downtown and harbored hopes of spending time with the cute little waitress. He'd taken more than casual notice of the four-foot, ten-inch charmer who sprinted around the restaurant, captivating everyone she batted her eyelashes at. His fondness for the young woman made it impossible to understand what drew her to a petty criminal like Clyde. He had plenty of company.

Barrow's prison records give us a more complete view of the man than grainy photographs, which often mislead the viewer by making the subject appear larger than he was in reality. The record describes him as a man of small stature—five foot, five or six inches tall—who had tiny feet and weighed only 127 pounds. Tattoos decorated his body like Christmas tree ornaments. Initials of an alias adorned his left arm (EBW for Elvin Williams). The letters USN over a naval shield motif covered the inner portion of his right forearm, and a portrait of a girl's head with the name Grace flew like a flag on the outer surface of the same limb.

Some have described the man as handsome, but in this humble writer's opinion, ol' Clyde's face had a somewhat pinched, ferret-like quality about it. He had brown eyes, a medium (brown) complexion, and brown hair. Almost everything about him seemed to be brown. For Ted Hinton to be surprised by the lovely Bonnie's choice in men should make complete sense to just about anybody.

Anyway, ol' Clyde despised prison, and about a month into his stay in Waco's calaboose, Bonnie committed what could arguably have been her first criminal act by smuggling him a pistol. He made maximum use of the weapon, escaped, and hoofed it for the safety of Middletown, Ohio, where he was promptly recaptured little more than a week later. Tried and quickly found guilty, the state sentenced the escaped convict to fourteen years of hard labor and sent him to Eastham Prison Farm in Crockett where he spent most of the next two years.

It should be noted here that hard labor did not include such modern-day muscle-kinking back-breakers as schlepping burgers, checking groceries, selling salads in a restaurant, or stocking potato chips down at the local supermarket. No, there once existed a time when hard labor meant exactly that. Prison road gangs dug ditches with picks and long-handled shovels. Convicts worked like sled dogs on state-run farms where all digging, chopping, weeding, and cultivating also got done by hand. They broke rocks, cut timber, hauled logs, and hand-picked cotton and peas. Blister city dudes!

Ol' Clyde's aversion to such fun and games ran so deep that he paid a fellow jailbird to chop off two of his toes with a double-bit axe. This proved an amazingly stupid act of desperation, because about a heartbeat later, in February 1932, he was awarded a general parole and hobbled back to the loving arms of his sweet Texas rosebud on crutches.

The panting lovers immediately picked up where they left off with their romance and set out on a crime spree that has seen no modern equal in the more than eighty years since. They started by robbing a string of grocery stores, gas stations, and small-town banks.

Some have used the harshness of the times to romanticize and justify Bonnie and Clyde's behavior. That great social experiment called Prohibition had recently ended, and the country hit rock bottom with the Depression at about the same time their little Texas two-step started. Crime statistics from 1933, extrapolated out to reflect a doubling in population (keep in mind that these figures are in no way offered as absolute scientific reality), would give us a modern-day yearly equivalent of more than 24,000 murders, 6,000 kidnappings, 100,000 robberies, and 200,000 assaults in addition to those we already witness. In Texas alone, if the figures come anywhere close to holding true, we'd have 2,000 homicides, 1,700 of them the result of gunfights. Texas and America's modern antigun contingent would have a collective stroke.

No doubt about it, criminal behavior, and the notoriety of people involved in such activity, enjoyed a form of popularity unlike any seen before or since. Commonly known thieves and star-quality killers included the likes of John Dillinger, Al Capone, "Pretty Boy" Floyd, "Baby Face" Nelson, "Machine Gun" Kelly, and Ma Barker. These murderers and bank robbers competed with Bonnie and Clyde for newspaper headlines, Movie-Tone News feature status, and motion picture biographies, but none managed the devoted following inspired by our sweet Texas duo.

In March 1932 the moon-eyed lovers, with their new partner, Raymond Hamilton, attempted a theft that resulted in Bonnie's capture and incarceration in the Kaufman, Texas, jail. Barely a month later the gang first made national headlines with the robbery and murder of a sixty-year-old grocer named J. W. Bucher of Hillsboro, a town of about 3,000 souls north of Waco. A girl, described as light-haired, assisted in Clyde's late-night party and pulled a gun on Bucher. The poor man made the mistake of trying to wrestle her pistol away and died a brutal death in the presence of his wife because of it. Clyde shot him D.O.S. (Dead On the Spot).

Martha Bucher identified Barrow from police photos. Her description of the light-haired girl sounded suspiciously like the lovely Bonnie, but there remains some mystery as to the female stickup artist's true identity. Seems that Bonnie was still locked up in the Kaufman pokey at the time—or at least she was supposed to be.

After a Kaufman grand jury no-billed Bonnie, she returned home and swore to her mother that Clyde Barrow was a thing of the past, dust on her shoes, nothing but a fading memory. Well, that seems to have lasted about a week, and on August 5, Clyde, his buddy Raymond Hamilton, a woman thought to be Bonnie, and several other close friends, attended a dance near Atoka in modern-day Oklahoma.

Sometime during the course of the evening's drinking and prancing, Clyde and Hamilton got into an argument and, like all close friends, family members, or business associates, stepped outside to duke it out. Deputy Sheriff E. C. Moore tried to break up the fight and was assaulted by the ubiquitous light-haired girl who accompanied Barrow. Moore tried to arrest the girl and got promptly shot dead for his efforts. When the sheriff, a gentleman named Maxwell, attempted to assist his fallen deputy, the gunmen blasted him out of his boots. He died a few days later.

For the next several months, Bonnie and her sweet Baboo ripped up and down the highways and byways of Texas, Oklahoma, Missouri, and New Mexico with absolutely no regard for law enforcement officials or seeming fear of the possibility they might be captured. They continued to rob small banks, mom-and-pop groceries, and gas stations. During the entire period from the murder of J. W. Bucher till their ultimate reward less than two years later, they never managed a theft larger than $1,500. If there ever existed a living definition of two-bit hoods, the Barrow gang had to be it.

In spite of such a poor monetary showing when compared to the other legendary gangsters of the era, the Barrow bunch still managed to push all the other thugs, rascals, and reprobates off the front pages of the country's newspapers with their exploits. They did it by killing people. Plain and simple, murder made them famous. Most specifically, the murder of law enforcement types seemed to be their forte.

Sometime after the August bloodshed in Oklahoma, Raymond Hamilton and the rest of the gang parted company. Unfortunately for dear ol' Raymond, a sweet young thing he'd been seeing turned him over to the law, and they dragged him back to Texas for trial. A jury of his peers took umbrage at his life of robbery, mayhem, and murder and sent the unrepentant killer to Huntsville for 263 years. When he complained of headaches and said he didn't think he could serve that long, the judge handed him two aspirin and told him to take one every 130 years. (Okay, okay! So I made up the part about the aspirin.)

Anyway, on October 11, 1932, Bonnie and her boyfriend cruised into Sherman and robbed a poor ex-cowboy turned grocer named Howard Hall. Hall, somewhat elderly by this time, complained when Clyde pushed a pistol into the old man's gut so hard it hurt. The bandit, ever the gentleman, backed up, apologized, laughed, and shot the antique cowpoke twice. The happy couple then spent a few minutes shopping for groceries, always making sure to step over the oozing corpse of Mr. Hall, ate a few sandwiches, and drove merrily away in a brand-new Ford. A stunned clerk identified the killers, and fingerprints found at the scene offered proof of the shaken man's powers of observation.

Their next homicide took place in Temple on December 5, 1932. Doyle Johnson, a lumber salesman, had barely settled into his easy chair for a bit of relaxation with the evening paper when he heard his car being cranked up. He looked out the window in time to see the second most expensive thing he'd ever purchased in his entire life being driven off by a man and followed by another car piloted by—that's right folks—a light-haired woman.

Doyle burst through the front door and sprinted across his lawn while being shot at a number of times by the woman, jumped onto the running board of his own auto, and grabbed the thief by the throat. The strangling driver gasped for air, placed a pistol against Mr. Johnson's forehead, and fired. He was dead when he hit the ground. His widow and a group of other witnesses identified Bonnie and Clyde as the killers.

Almost exactly a month later, the murderous brigands visited Dallas and hatched a plot to break Raymond Hamilton out of the jail he'd been transferred to down in Hillsboro. Local law dogs somehow discovered the couple were in town and set up a friendly homecoming ambush or two. The lawmen staked out the homes of several of Clyde and Bonnie's friends and waited.

On January 6, 1933, Deputy Sheriff Malcom Davis jumped from behind shrubbery near the home of Mrs. Lillie McBride with guns drawn as Barrow approached. Davis demanded that the desperado disarm and throw up his hands. Clyde had absolutely no intention of being captured again and returned to prison. Hey, he was missing two toes and wasn't about to cut off any more. He shot Davis deader'n Davy Crockett. Bonnie put the pedal to the metal and tore away from their most current carnage with Clyde riding on the running board.

The killers didn't stop bookin' it till they got to South Joplin, Missouri, where they rented a cottage and entertained Clyde's brother Buck, his wife Blanche, and gang member W. D. Jones. The bungalow took on all the aspects of a 1930s roadhouse with plenty of liquor, loud music, and rowdy behavior.

For about three months the bandits managed to do their looting and pillaging without killing anyone. But their South Joplin neighbors started to get suspicious of the pair and their friends, because of some rather strange habits. People reported seeing stacks of assorted license plates lying around in the floor of their rambunctious neighbor's garage. The men tended to vanish for long periods and reappear at strange hours. The women rarely left the house, and complaints started to filter into the local police department because of the earsplitting, drunken parties that seemed to go on nonstop. The phrase car thieves got thrown around quite a bit as most residents came to feel that dangerous people had invaded their bucolic locale.

On April 13, 1933, after numerous complaints, a pair of Missouri State Highway Patrolmen gave the house a cursory look and returned later with some Joplin police officers to do a more detailed investigation. Indications are that the five lawmen suspected the occupants of the house were in fact the Barrow gang. Given that suspicion, their actions bordered on the demented. A local constable named Harryman boldly walked up to within ten feet of the garage and was promptly sent to kingdom come by well-placed blasts from both barrels of a shotgun.

All hell broke loose. General gunfire from both sides of the dispute turned the quiet neighborhood into a war zone. The Missouri cops made the same mistake all the other law enforcement types had up until then. Very simply put, they failed to understand the extent and power of Clyde Barrow's arsenal or his willingness to die rather than go back to prison. Those .38 caliber police service revolvers couldn't match the deadliness of Clyde's favorite weapon, the military version of a Browning automatic rifle.

For the uninitiated, this weapon is still one of the most powerful, devastating, and dependable pieces of armament ever invented for tactical infantry use. It can lay down a withering field of offensive or defensive fire. Rustic police departments of the early 1930s had nothing in their respective equipment racks that even came close to comparing to such a weapon. Barrow's love of the gun is easily discernible by the number of photographs in existence which show him holding one of several used during his and Bonnie's two-year spree and the fact that he had three of them in his possession when he died. Even a highly trained, well-equipped, modern SWAT team would retreat in the face of fire from a B.A.R.

In spite of a fairly spirited offensive barrage from the remaining Missouri lawmen, Bonnie, Clyde, Buck, Blanche, and ol' W. D. managed to make it to their car, kill detective Harry McGinnis as he attempted to help his fallen friend, and escape with little more than a few nuisance scratches.

Afterward, during a thorough search of the bungalow, a reporter found and developed several rolls of film that contained images that

*Photos from a 1933 Joplin, Missouri, wanted poster for Clyde Barrow. No mention is made of Bonnie Parker's part in the gun battle that ended with the deaths of Detective Harry McGinnis and Constable J. W Harryman on the poster.* Courtesy Texas Ranger Hall of Fame and Museum. Waco, Texas

have since become some of the easiest to identify in American criminal history. The most recognizable of the photos pictured Bonnie swaggeringly posed with her left foot on the bumper of a car, pistol in hand, her tiny mouth stretched out of shape by a huge cigar. The brazen-hussy, spraddle-legged, stogie-chomping stance did more to damage the gang's Robin Hood image with common folk than anything law enforcement could have ever managed.

Newspapers all over the country ran front-page copies of the snapshots. Wanted posters with the image of the cigar-puffing Bonnie covered the country in a blizzard of paper. She later claimed the picture was a joke, but the image of a slutty-looking, rough-as-a-cob gun moll stuck and probably did as much to insure her eventual doom as any of the crimes she committed. Within weeks of the Joplin shoot-out, people from Bangor, Maine, to San Diego, California, could easily distinguish every member of Bonnie and Clyde's band of incredibly lucky killers.

In June 1933 the now famous female hoodlum's luck began to slide away like a bobsled with no brakes. She was badly burned after Clyde ran through a detour sign near Wellington, Oklahoma, and wrecked their car. From that point on, Clyde often had to carry Bonnie to their automobile, and she walked with a decided limp even after months of recovery.

Following a few weeks convalescence for her near fatal injuries, the gang robbed a grocery store in Fayetteville, Arkansas, and murdered Marshal H. D. Humphrey of the tiny town of Alma when he tried to stop them. By this point, the Barrow bunch had slaughtered nine people Alma—six of them peace officers in the performance of their sworn duties—in little more than a year. Additionally, every time a similar crime got committed anywhere in the southern half of the United States, Bonnie and her boyfriend got the blame and notoriety, whether they deserved it or not. When H. D. Humphrey assumed room temperature, most people believed Bonnie and Clyde were responsible for more than twenty killings. The tide of goodwill, tacit acceptance, and public sympathy they had enjoyed in the past began to rapidly evaporate as law-abiding people finally realized the full extent of the danger loose amongst them.

In spite of all the previous gunplay, robbery, and general insanity, nothing could have prepared a naive America for the events of the week that unfolded on July 28, 1933, in Platte City, Missouri. More than a score of state, local, and federal lawmen surrounded the fugitives in a motel and tried to block their flight by parking an armored car in front of the garage. Clyde's Brownings shot the supposed impregnable vehicle into pieces and forced the policemen's retreat during a blistering gun battle that once again ended with the gang's escape.

Embarrassed authorities put considerable effort into the chase this time and caught up with the desperate bunch again four days later in a park outside Dexter, Iowa. A posse, made up of more than a hundred policemen, members of the National Guard, and local farmers, launched a massive assault on the desperate killers as they tried to rest and recuperate from injuries incurred during the Platte City raid. Buck Barrow was captured and died of numerous wounds ten days later. His wife, Blanche, surrendered after being shot in the eye. But the bumbling pursuers still managed to allow Bonnie, Clyde, and W. D. to slip through their fingers in spite of a brutal barrage of gunfire.

If a single event in her brief, savage, and bloody career can be pointed to as the beginning of the end for Bonnie Parker, her participation in Raymond Hamilton's brazen escape from Eastham State Farm has to be it. On the morning of January 16, 1934, guards led a prison work crew into cotton fields in the Trinity River Valley. Hamilton and another convict, Joe Palmer, quickly armed themselves with .45 caliber Colt pistols previously hidden behind a log by Barrow. Bonnie and Clyde sped up on a nearby highway, and the prisoners sprinted for the car and the possibility of freedom. General gunfire erupted from both sides. Guards and fleeing jailbirds burned powder at each other more than a hundred times. Barrow and Hamilton would later quibble over who fired the fatal shot that killed one of the prison guards. It really didn't matter. Hamilton, Henry Methvin, Joe Palmer, and W. H. Bybee managed to escape, and the entire crew of murderous gangsters deemed the operation a huge success.

Sorely provoked and personally enraged, Lee Simmons, head of the Texas State Prison System, petitioned then-governor Miriam (Ma) Ferguson and her husband, former governor Jim Ferguson, for authority to put a special investigator on the Barrow gang's trail. Simmons knew that whoever went after Bonnie and Clyde would do so at the risk of his own life. He had credible testimony that Barrow intended to go down shooting—previous behavior reinforced that attitude—and Bonnie had expressed her intent to die with him. Simmons and Texas's two-for-one governors quickly agreed on the right man for the job. Enter Frank Hamer.

In a day and age when the word legend gets thrown around to the point where modern automobile makers classify their quickly depreciating plastic and sheet metal efforts with the word, it might not be possible for most people to actually recognize a real one. Our human legends at the dawn of the new millennium tend to be of the dribbler, kicker, shooter, hitter, runner, singer, picker, dancer, rap-poet, or actor type. At the time of his entry into the Parker-Barrow story, Frank Hamer already enjoyed living legend status in law enforcement circles all over the United States and had the credentials to back it up.

His career started with the capture of a South Texas horse thief in 1905. He was a twenty-one-year-old ranch hand at the time. Sheriff D. S. Barker—much impressed with the young cowboy—recommended him for a slot with the Texas Rangers. In 1906 Hamer enlisted in Captain John H. Rogers's Company C and spent most of the next five years working the toughest part of the South Texas border. Along the way, he became well known as an expert shot, and the criminal element quickly recognized him as a man who should never be taken lightly. This first outing with the Rangers lasted till 1908, when he resigned and took on the job of city marshal for the violence-ridden town of Navasota. He renewed his relationship with the Rangers in 1911 and worked the lawless stretch of border from the Big Bend Country east all the way to the Gulf of Mexico. Arms smugglers, bootleggers, bandits, whores, killers, and thieves were thicker'n woodpeckers on a hackberry tree. Some grumbling about the use of force bubbled up from the criminal element, but most law-abiding people just ignored it, hit their knees at night, and thanked God for men like Ranger Frank Hamer.

A personal dispute over Governor Jim Ferguson's inclination to appoint just anyone who happened to be handy to the Ranger service led to Hamer's resignation in 1920 and a stint with the US Prohibition service where he rose to the rank of captain. During the period from 1922 to 1932, he was credited with cleaning up vicious boomtowns like

*Quintessential Texas Ranger Frank Hamer, the man who brought an end to Bonnie and Clyde's reign of terror, is pictured here in a more traditional setting than the machine guns, cars, and planes era of the 1930s that made his name a household word.* Courtesy Texas Ranger Hall of Fame and Museum. Waco, Texas

Mexia, Gander Slu, and Borger. His disgust with the Fergusons never abated, and in 1925 he resigned again when former governor Jim Ferguson's wife, Miriam, managed to get elected. The outcry over the decision and personal appeals from the Fergusons led to his return to the service a second time.

Hamer never backed down from a fight with those who chose to break the law, but in 1928 he made some powerful enemies when he exposed a murderous scheme by the Texas Bankers' Association. They announced a standing reward of $5,000 for any dead bank robber. Hamer discovered that people used the offer as an excuse to frame, track down, and kill any two-bit hoodlum available just to collect the money.

When he went public with his findings on the covert wickedness of the assassination for money plot, the public put so much pressure on the bankers that they relented and stopped the evil practice.

In 1932 Miriam Ferguson managed to get herself elected governor of Texas again, and Frank immediately retired from active duty with the Rangers while retaining his commission. By the time of his final departure in 1949, the old lawman had been involved in hundreds of gunfights, was believed to have killed as many as fifty-three men while on duty, and had been shot seventeen times and left in the dirt for dead at least four times. In spite of such valor, dedication to duty, and steadfast loyalty to the cause of law and order, a fairy-tale film version of Bonnie and Clyde's final two years treated Hamer in the shabbiest fashion. Warren Beatty should have been publicly slapped silly for his portrayal of a true Texas hero. When Lee Simmons put Hamer on Bonnie and Clyde's trail on February 10, 1934, they were dead people walking.

The killing of a single prison guard most certainly insured Bonnie Parker's place in a coffin, but the Grapevine murders on Easter Sunday 1934 nailed the lid shut. A confusing array of eyewitness accounts of the event make an airtight description of the scene virtually impossible. What's known for certain is that the gang had parked on a hill near Highway 114, and two motorcycle policemen—E. D. Wheeler and H. D. Murphy—stopped to investigate. Both men fell in a hail of gunfire after they dismounted and approached the vehicle, and someone—either a light-haired woman dressed in pants or an effeminate man—got out of the bandit's car and shot one of the injured officers in the face with a shotgun, then laughed, "Look-a-there, his head bounced just like a rubber ball." Enraged police officers pursued the murderers but couldn't catch them. Whiskey bottles found at the scene were covered with Bonnie and Clyde's fingerprints.

A few days after the Grapevine shootings, America's most notorious, itinerant killers committed their last murder. Sixty-three-year-old

Constable Cal Campbell and policeman Percy Boyd stopped and offered to help the hoodlums get their car out of the mud near Miami, Oklahoma. Barrow shotgunned Campbell. The friendly grandfather died on the spot. Bonnie and Henry Methvin opened fire on Boyd, who was still sitting in Campbell's car. They managed to put a crease in the stunned policeman's skull, forced him to help with their bogged-down automobile, then took him for a frenzied fourteen-hour ride before finally turning him loose.

Bonnie was later quoted as saying, "We liked him. When we let him out, we gave him a new shirt and tie and expense money back home. He asked me, 'Bonnie, what shall I tell the world when I go back?' And I said, 'Tell them I don't smoke cigars!' He did it too. It was in all the Oklahoma newspapers." From that moment on, Bonnie and Clyde spent every waking hour running for their lives.

On Sunday April 29, 1934, Ruth Warren watched from her kitchen window in Kansas as Clyde Barrow jumped from the running board of a passing Plymouth, ran to her beautiful new Ford Deluxe V8, started it—with keys she'd left in the ignition—and sped away. She wouldn't see her $785 investment again till three months later. The bullet-riddled, blood-splattered car, motor number 649198, looked like her grandmother's bent-up flour sifter.

Meanwhile, human bloodhound Frank Hamer was hot on their trail. Movie, and some written, versions of what happened on May 23, 1934, usually portray lowlife scum who betray Bonnie and Clyde by acting as bait for the ambush. Some claim that Irvin Methvin—father of Henry Methvin, who supposedly lived nearby—acted as an involuntary decoy. He was, or perhaps wasn't, chained to a tree while his broken-down truck blocked the roadway. My description of the events of that day is taken directly from the one man who should know what happened—Frank Hamer. His personal narration of that bloody morning can be found in his famous Jenkins and Frost biography.

According to the old lawman, virtually all criminals kept a secret drop used for communications that couldn't be traced through the regular mail. Clyde's was under a broken piece of board, near a stump, on a side road about eight miles from Plain Dealing, Louisiana. On the night of May 22, Hamer and five other lawmen hid themselves in the woods a few yards across the road and waited. Among the posse members was Ted Hinton, Bonnie's former suitor from her days at the American Cafe. He'd quit the post office and taken a deputy's position with the Dallas County Sheriff's department. Others in the party were M. T. Gault, Bob Alcorn, Louisiana Sheriff Henderson Jordan, and his deputy—a man named Curtis Oakley.

At approximately 9:10 in the morning, a gray Ford sedan stopped near the stump. Hamer's party recognized the stolen automobile and its occupants. Barrow slipped the car into low gear and left the engine idling. When commanded to "Stick 'em up!" both desperadoes grabbed for weapons and the blasting began. The car started moving forward, and the shooting intensified in an effort to stop what appeared to be another escape. By the time the smoke and dust finally cleared, automatic rifles, pistols, and shotguns had punched 167 holes in Ruth Warren's pride and joy. Hamer approached the car first and pulled the driver's door open. Clyde's bullet-riddled body flopped onto the ground at his feet. Bonnie slumped so far forward her head rested between her knees. Autopsies on the two killers would reveal that each had been hit more than fifty times.

The old Texas Ranger described the car as "nothing but an arsenal on wheels." Clyde's personal armory included three Browning automatic rifles, two sawed-off shotguns, ten pistols (seven of them .45 Colt automatics), one hundred clips of twenty cartridges each for the B.A.R.s, and 3,000 rounds of other types of loose ammunition. It's a miracle Ruth Warren's car didn't explode.

If anyone thought gettin' dead was the end of Bonnie and Clyde, they couldn't have been more wrong. When the car and bodies arrived in

*The front page of the* Dallas Morning News *dated May 24, 1934, screamed with headlines and stories that detailed Frank Hamer's ambush end to the bloody lives of Bonnie and Clyde. Pictured in the middle of the page are top row (l-r) Clyde Barrow, Bonnie Parker, and Frank Hamer. Bottom row (l-r) Deputy Sheriffs Bob Alcorn and Ted Hinton. Others who participated but are not pictured included M. T. Gault, also a former Texas Ranger, Sheriff Henderson Jordan of Bienville Parish, Louisiana, and his deputy Curtis Oakley.* Author's collection

Arcadia, Louisiana, people started to gather, gawk, and demand their rights to see the dead criminals. Quicker'n God could get the news, the crowd grew to something more than six thousand people of every kind, type, and stripe imaginable. One group of rednecks mobbed up around the bullet-riddled automobile and went to ripping and tearing at anything they could cart away. People fought and argued over gruesome mementos spattered with blood or brains. The shattered side and rear windows were torn out of the car and hundreds of the appallingly weird carried away bits of glass from the soon to be infamous death car to commemorate their brush with infamy.

Other folks, who can only be categorized as morbidly inquisitive in the extreme, even managed to gain entry to the tiny room where the embalming took place, and several had to be removed when they fainted. Those who couldn't get close enough to the action in Arcadia raced back to the scene of the ambush and picked the area clean of spent shell casings, bullets lodged in trees, and pieces of the shattered automobile abandoned in the roadway.

The bodies of Bonnie Parker and Clyde Barrow were eventually transported to Dallas where thousands more viewed their pitiful remains. On May 25 Barrow's family buried him next to his brother Buck in the West Dallas Cemetery on a hillside a short distance from his boyhood home. The crowd nearly overwhelmed the family and almost pushed some of them into the grave with Clyde. Captain Hamer attended the funeral but left in disgust when ghoulish souvenir hunters snatched up everything on or around the grave that could be carried away.

On numerous occasions Bonnie had indicated to her mother that she wanted to spend eternity next to her lovin' man. Mama wouldn't allow it. Mrs. Emma Parker has been quoted as saying, "Now that she's dead, she's all mine. I don't want her buried with Clyde. He had her while she was alive." On Saturday, May 26, amid near public hysteria, Mrs. Parker buried her daughter in a steel casket at Fishtrap Cemetery.

～～

It took time and a hardworking lawyer to help Ruth Warren get her car back. With brain matter and gore still in vivid evidence, she drove it to Shreveport, loaded it on a truck, and hauled it back to Kansas. Her neighbors almost had a collective cat while the hideous thing sat in her driveway. She leased the now infamous death car to John Castle, who exhibited it all over the country. Charles Stanley bought it from the Warrens, and for almost a decade Bonnie and Clyde's last ride drew sizable crowds everywhere it appeared. The gruesome exhibit was so successful that scores of fakes also pulled in crowds and made lots of money.

Ted Toddy purchased the genuine, true-life, real honest-to-God Bonnie and Clyde Death Car in 1952 for just under $15,000. Toddy must have been an astute businessman. He put it in storage and no one saw it again until fifteen years later when Warren Beatty's fairy tale of a movie broke box office records. Toddy made over $1 million dragging the bullet-peppered piece of junk to movie theaters, state fairs, and just about anyplace else large enough to park it and charge for admission. He raked in ten times more money on that shattered shell of twisted metal and glass than all the Barrow gang's robberies combined. Your author remembers seeing it at the Arkansas State Fair in 1968. Or maybe that one was a fake. Who knows?

The romantic stories, legends, and outright lies about the entire Bonnie and Clyde episode have grown, expanded, mutated, and been told and retold so many times over the past years that people are still fascinated by their bloody lives and shocking deaths. Several brand-new books on their overly examined escapades have hit the shelves, and others are said to be in the works. Recently a sold-out tour of more than sixty people visited all the Dallas, Texas, sites where the star-crossed lovers lived or visited or shot the hell out of somebody. When asked why he thought people still wanted to see such places, tour guide John Neal Phillips replied, "There's something in all of us that wants to live vicariously through someone who's done something we'd never do. And there's something about a young man and young woman who stuck together like they did. They knew they were gonna die." Hard to argue with such reasoning, except to note that a sizable segment of any population suffers from terminal heebie-jeebie weird inquisitiveness and never misses a chance to show up when morbid curiosity rears its ugly, many tentacled head. Why people would want to stomp around on Bonnie Parker's pitiful little grave until not one blade of grass can grow simply passes all understanding of most folks, including this author.

# CHAPTER 14

— •◦• —

## IT'S SAD, SO SAD
### Janis Joplin

As was mentioned briefly in the previous chapter, the quality of leg-end has changed dramatically over the past hundred fifty years. Prior to the advent of "talking" movies, the status reserved for those who achieved such vaunted significance tended to be reserved for men and women whose accomplishments could easily be recognized in noteworthy fields such as medicine, politics, religion, science, exploration, philosophy, or language and letters. Today our "heroes" tend to be those who dribble it, kick it, shoot it, hit it, throw it, and run with it, or the people who sing, dance, mug for the cameras, and otherwise perform in the hundreds of motion pictures and television presentations that come to us begging for our approval, and money, every day. In the telling words of a character from a recent, critically acclaimed film, in the America of the late twentieth or early twenty-first century you're just nobody if you're not on television or in the movies.

On a steaming, clammy evening, typical of the Texas gulf coast in August 1970, a chauffeur-driven Chrysler limo delivered a twenty-seven-year-old female living legend to the Tenth Anniversary Reunion of the Port Arthur, Texas, Thomas Jefferson High School graduating class of 1960. She oozed sloppily out of the car's door enveloped in a cloud of legally dubious gray-blue smoke dressed in a Ringling Brothers-Barnum and Bailey outfit of purple and white satin. The costume was accentuated with a plethora of pink and blue feathers that decorated a tangled mass of hair and gave her head the appearance of a bizarre stop-action photograph of a psychedelic explosion. Her bare feet were clad in the scantiest of sandals, and enough rings and bracelets decorated her fingers and arms to fill the sales counters of several Los Angeles head shops. She boogied from the street into the closed arms and all-enveloping mists of her past, accompanied by an entourage composed of equal parts weirdness, goofy psychological need, and just plain confusion. Her actions and appearance immediately managed to give a king-sized dose of Texas pissoffedness to a sizable number of those who had graduated with her and still lived in the little port city.

Former classmates and local critics, who witnessed her arrival and subsequent behavior, said later she was totally wasted, but that most of the other attendees forgave actions on her part they would normally have considered less than commendable. However, some felt, and still feel to this day, that she should have been arrested on the spot for her drugged and drunken conduct.

No one knows exactly why Janis Lyn Joplin even deigned to attend that paradigm of middle-class one-upmanship. There is no existing indication she had a "good time" that night. This in spite of the fact that some former members of her graduating class who had never spoken to her in high school, or had missed a chance to call her horrible things to her face, fell all over themselves to suck up to a now-famous woman they wouldn't generally have bothered to spit on if she had burst into ten-foot-high flames before their very faces.

If we can believe her own words, a few weeks prior to the celebration she appeared on a popular late-night television talk show and said she planned to attend the party, "Just to jam it up their asses. I'm going down there with my fur hat and my feathers and see all those kids who are still working in gas stations and driving dry cleaning trucks while I'm making $50,000 a night."

Her attitude toward the experiences of her teenaged years isn't that unusual for famous people. In a wonderful book published in the 1970s named *Is There Life After High School,* Ralph Keyes pointed out that Mia Farrow never forgot or forgave when all the girls at the prom except her were asked to dance. Charles Schultz remembered that every cartoon he submitted to the yearbook staff got rejected, and Warren Beatty never missed a chance to remind anyone within shouting distance that he turned down ten college football scholarships to pursue acting, thus ridiculing his high school heroics while at the same time reminding us of his status as the big man on campus.

Whatever the reason for Janis's questionable attendance that hot August night, close friends have testified that she left even further depressed by the reception she received from her former friends, family, and hometown. Two months later, on October 5, 1970, she died from an overdose of heroin and alcohol that could have dropped a range-crazed longhorn steer in its tracks. A fiery life filled with sex, drugs, and rock and roll killed her as surely as if she'd taken a pistol, put it to her head, and pulled the trigger. The moment talking heads on network news programs announced her sad and lonely departure from this life, the so-called "legend" of that desperately depressed and needy young woman was forever woven into the fabric of our popular culture.

Janis came into the world on January 19, 1943. Her father, Seth Joplin, left college before finishing and worked as an operations engineer in Port Arthur's Texaco refinery. Her mother, Dorothy, kept house, taught Sunday school, and eventually took a job as registrar at a local business college. They had been married seven years when their beautiful baby girl was born.

In the beginning Janis displayed few of the characteristics you'd expect from the future queen of quirkiness and unconventional behavior. Her childhood can best be described as painfully normal to the point of being downright bland. Typical of most southern girls, she attended church with her mother, eventually taught beginner Sunday school classes as a teenager, and sang in the church choir. Even at that early age her voice was such that she could bring authority to different musical presentations. The church choir director recognized her gift and used her vibrant contralto voice for alto and soprano presentations. A born performer, she never missed a chance to take part in local play productions and displayed an astonishing skill as an amateur painter. Existing examples of her artwork could easily be interpreted as exposing her as a talented artist and quite a different young woman from most of the girls in little ol' conservative Port Arthur of the 1950s. She was bright, considered pretty by boys her age, outgoing, friendly, and seemed to have a talent for just about anything she wanted to do.

Then, around the age of thirteen, something awful happened to Janis. Acne ravaged her soft southern features and forever changed her self-perception. For those fresh-faced folks who somehow manage to get past puberty having never suffered this particular calamity, there is simply no way to describe its emotional impact. Her teenage catastrophe, coupled with failures to win local art contests, led to feelings of rejection and disappointment so intense that she stopped painting—an avocation she dearly loved.

By the time she arrived in high school, her weight had ballooned, the skin problems were about as bad as anyone can imagine, and she had begun to dress like a man. In what must have seemed like an overnight transformation, she went from a child who did anything she could to please everyone around her to a full-fledged rebellious misfit openly seeking the label of outsider.

At a time when "nice" girls didn't dare voice anything like a radical opinion, Janis let everyone within earshot know exactly how she felt about any subject they wanted to discuss and did it in language so hot, vulgar, and nasty it could fry bacon in an iron skillet. She openly criticized the racist treatment of blacks, which caused gangs of abusive boys to dog her trail in the hallways and shout racial slurs as she made her way from class to class. Her mother was appalled. Her father could do nothing with his rebellious daughter and has been quoted as saying that Janis was the first fire-breathing revolutionary their little town had ever seen.

In the eleventh grade she discovered a degree of acceptance with a small group of students who read Kerouac, Burroughs, and other "Beat" writers and roamed from Port Arthur to New Orleans haunting bistros and nightclubs in their never-ending search for acceptance. During these raids Janis discovered music from all over the southern states and Caribbean. Country-western, Cajun, soul, gospel, the blues, and jazz began to rattle around in her untrained head and soon her consumption of recordings by Odetta, Bessie Smith, Willie Mae Thornton, and others resulted in an almost supernatural ability to imitate virtually anything she heard on a record. Friends from that period have said that she could sing every song Odetta ever laid down on vinyl.

Her nonconformist, antisocial behavior, which she referred to as "beatnik" because no other descriptive term existed at the time, continued unabated, drove former acquaintances away, and alienated everyone who felt that a "nice" girl didn't run with the "kinds of people" Janis now counted as friends. By the time she graduated from Jefferson High, her vocabulary of foul language, shocking dress, reputation for sexual adventurism, and early signs of an addictive personality (by way of frequent drunkenness) led classmates to universally refer to her in the most dreaded insult a southern woman can hear—slut. Absent any "real" friends, unable to find dates for school functions, and deeply ashamed of her scarred face and mannish figure, she worsened her situation by responding in kind and never missed a chance to contemptuously insult those who openly passed judgment on her behavior or beliefs.

Upon graduation her parents packed her up and shipped her off to Los Angeles to visit with her mother's sisters who lived near Venice Beach. California was just beginning to bask in the glow of a national reputation as being the place where all the fruits and nuts went when the rest of the country screened them out of the more conservative areas. Venice Beach had the local reputation of being where California's, and thereby the entire country's, weirdest tended to congregate. Most likely Janis's parents felt that some distance from the pain of Port Arthur and new surroundings might bring about a return of the sweet-natured daughter they once knew. Well kiss my grits, boys and girls, they couldn't have made a poorer parental decision. For the first time in her life she met "real" beatniks, and the love beads and leather boots crowd didn't miss a chance to shovel "real" drugs into the hands of someone who needed them about like another hole in the head. When she made it back to Texas, her friends were astonished by the possibilities she glowingly painted and were impressed all to hell and gone with actual California-grown marijuana, something they had heard stories about but never actually seen.

The social consciousness of the sixties now came to the young people of the country in the form of speeches by John F. Kennedy, and Janis took him at his word. For a time she attended Lamar State College of Technology at Beaumont, but found her situation almost a duplicate of high school. Branded a misfit in both places, she fled to the University of Texas at Austin in the summer of 1962 to study her first love, art. But her career as a student suffered from the very beginning, and she quickly found congenial company in the society of counterculture groups who sang folk songs and performed in nightclubs near the university's campus.

She fronted for a little band that called itself The Waller Creek Boys and had finally begun to gain the acceptance she always craved while singing at Threadgill's, a former gas station that had been converted into a nightspot and beer-joint for music lovers and full-bore party animals. Her quickly growing reputation as a performer filled the tiny place with an eclectic crowd of fans composed of friends, students, and

*Janis Joplin got her start on the road to fame and riches at Kenneth Threadgill's restaurant in Austin. The original eatery has retained its traditional look and is still the center of Austin's live music scene.* Author's collection

young appreciative Austinites. The famed roadhouse's owner, Kenneth Threadgill, gave Janis the encouragement she needed and became a lifelong friend. For a time she was a hit, but not on campus. Unthinking, unfeeling redneck frat boys nominated her as their candidate in the annual Ugliest Man on Campus contest, and worse than that, when all the votes were counted, she won. Some claim she just laughed it off to cover the pain of such meanness, but friend Powell St. John has said that the cruelty hit her so hard it was one of the few times he ever saw her break down and cry.

In 1963 she and good buddy Chet Helms left Texas and headed for the much more tolerant climate of San Francisco. They hitchhiked for fifty hours. When they arrived, for the first time in years, Janis no longer stood out like a sore thumb. She'd barely had time to visit the best-known hippie areas when she started performing at a joint named Coffee and Confusion. Within weeks freely available drugs of every type and description caused her consumption to spiral out of control. Things really got hairy when she started dating a man who made a living selling speed, and over the next two years her friends became concerned for her health and life. Local audiences showered her with attention, but her addiction began to push the singing aside and reduced her to a withered scarecrow that weighed less than ninety pounds. She came nigh unto dying by the time the hat got passed and friends forced a bus ticket back to Texas into her shaking hands.

It should never be said that the woman didn't try to stay straight. She cleaned herself up, dressed like the wife of a Baptist song leader, strictly stayed away from recreational chemicals, and through a combination of family support and fear of dying if she relapsed, managed to stay sober for a time. But frilly dresses and big hair were a constant reminder that she had sold out and was well on the way to being converted back to the outgrown small-town culture she hated with a vengeance and that hated her with equal ferocity.

Safe, dull Port Arthur once again proved no match for the siren call of San Francisco. In 1966, when Chet Helms invited her to front for a new group he managed called Big Brother and the Holding Company, she rushed back to the City by the Bay and what would be four years of dazzling, roller-coaster success, worldwide recognition—and early death. People being what they were, and are, so-called "friends" back home who were aware of her universal deficiency when it came to sexual preference started spreading the story that Janis was Big Brother.

The new band's first performance at the Avalon Ballroom was a monster hit with the San Francisco crowd. From that night on, Janis's stage persona drew huge audiences of people who danced in the aisles, swayed, clapped, and shouted encouragement through dense clouds of smoke from their particular crop of wacky weed. It seemed to those free-loving but angst-ridden folks that her actions on stage and vocal renditions pleaded for their participation and unrestrained affection. And the truth of it was that Janis not only loved but also craved such audience involvement.

Better-known groups were stunned with the power and passion she exhibited on stage. Bob Weir of the Grateful Dead once watched her voice on an oscilloscope and said that she had the amazing ability to belt out seven notes at the same time. In his opinion a good singer could hit two, a great singer three and maybe four. B. B. King, who considered Janis a genius, believed he could hear two people when she sang. She seemed to have the uncanny ability to produce a clear, distinct, and tremulous duet from her amazingly flexible throat. An astonishing feat when you consider how much cigarette smoke, whiskey, drugs, and other such detrimentally noxious crap got passed over her vocal cords.

In very short order, her name became linked with better-known pickers and grinners of the time, and she made the fateful decision to stay in San Francisco. As a group, the new band moved into a commune in the Haight-Ashbury area where everyone used drugs like there was no tomorrow and uninhibited do-it-with-anybody-handy sex was fun and free and the variety of new partners seemingly endless. In spite of all her good intentions, she slid back into her old habits. Drug and alcohol abuse quickly grew to gargantuan proportions.

For those of you out there in reader land who don't remember April through August of 1967, pop culture writers and those whose opinions everyone considered essential to their everyday existence dubbed it the "Summer of Love." Their silly label stuck in spite of the fact that it and the following year might well have been the most chaotic period in peacetime American history. The Detroit race riots of July were followed eight months later by Lyndon Johnson's stunning announcement to the nation that he would not (and he didn't leave any doubt about it) run for reelection. Martin Luther King's April 1968 assassination was followed by more riots, death, and destruction, and the entire insane period got topped off with the murder of Robert Kennedy.

In June 1967, just prior to the carnage in Detroit, Janis and Big Brother got the break of a lifetime when they were invited to perform at the Monterey Pop Festival. Their stiffest competition in the Bay Area, Jefferson Airplane and the Grateful Dead, also made appearances along with Otis Redding and The Who. A wild new personality on the scene named Jimi Hendrix set fire to his guitar just before she and her aston-ished friends took the stage. Several were heard to mutter something along the lines of "How in the hell are we gonna follow something like that?" as they stepped out in front of a fired-up crowd of fifty thou-sand wild-eyed, tie-died, French-fried California music hounds. Janis grabbed the microphone and literally blew everyone out of their psyche-delic beads, boots, and sandals. Her rendition of Big Mama Thornton's "Ball and Chain" brought the crowd to a screaming stomping frenzy and overnight gained her the attention of the entire nation for the first time.

The single greatest benefit of that performance was the impression it made on Clive Davis, an executive with Columbia Records, who heard Janis and couldn't wait to get her in a studio making music for his com-pany. He could see the promise under all the rough edges and imme-diately went to work extracting her and Big Brother from contractual agreements with an outfit named Mainstream Records. It ended up cost-ing him two hundred thousand dollars—a seriously substantial amount of geetus in that day and age—about three million simoleons in the stuff folks who now work for a living make in the new, and better, millennium. Janis had just turned twenty-five.

By February 1968 she could easily have been considered a bona fide star in the pop music heavens, on top of the world, or at least that's the way it seemed to those on the outside looking in. Close friends have spo-ken of her astonishment at being paid huge fees for doing what she used to do for free and be laughed at for in the process. Others expressed equal amazement that anyone could perform while consuming several fifths of Southern Comfort corn squeezings like they were just a few bottles of grape soda pop.

Young men and women who had always existed on the fringes of high school and college society flocked to her concerts and openly expressed the opinion that Janis spoke to them on a level that no other entertainer had even bothered to explore. As far as they were concerned the pain of people ignored by the rich, famous, and beautiful came through her emotionally wrenching, alcohol-saturated performances.

In June 1968 she and Big Brother went into an L.A. recording studio and came out with an album named *Cheap Thrills.* From then on everyone wanted to talk to her, take her picture, shake her hand, just breathe the sacred air surrounding the newly famous first woman of rock and roll, Janis Joplin. Her thrill at such attention resulted in the now legendary Francesco Scavullo photo session. His pictures of the celebrated singer are some of the best ever taken of a woman who ended up being one of the most photographed people in the world at the time.

But lurking behind all the overwrought hype and hoopla was a manager named Albert Grossman. He encouraged his now popular singer to dump her San Francisco band for a more versatile and disciplined group. By then members of Big Brother were feeling the sting of being relegated to the status of nothing more than support group for Janis, and it didn't sit well with some of them. They were pissed when she left them, but most understood why she did it and looked to the future.

When she formed the Kozmic Blues Band, her fans roundly criticized the move. The stunned singer retreated further into her heroin addiction to cope with what she deemed a stinging rejection and her conflicted feeling about dismissing a group of close friends for the sake of success. On top of everything else, the press began to delve into and devote way more print space to her drug abuse than they had in the past. And, according to friends, the necessity for midnight to daylight sessions to walk off overdoses became more frequent. Some even said that the drugs made the Janis that everyone liked disappear.

Didn't matter to the rest of the world, the good news just kept coming. In late 1968 *Jazz and Pop Magazine* voted her Best Female Vocalist of the Year. No doubt about it, Janis was now a genuine rock-and-roll star whose appeal crossed the Atlantic and resulted in a European tour in the summer of 1969. Being away from the drug scene in the states actually helped her, and there were those who held out some hope things might be looking up. In June she returned to the states, made another album, and did the TV talk show gig. Buttoned-down, club-tied Dick Cavett took a liking to Janis and even put the big preppy move on her. When asked about the incident, Cavett simply smiled knowingly, blushed like Blanche Du Bois, and said it was all very simple—they just liked each other. She must have been flattered, but evidently nothing came of it.

On August 16, 1969, she got herself good and juiced up for a performance and helicoptered in to a cow pasture on a farm near the tiny town of Woodstock in upstate New York. Passengers on the ride with her said that when she looked out the window and saw the crowd of 500,000 below, she almost passed out. No one could relate to an audience of that many people. Prior to Woodstock, no one could relate to anything where that many people showed up at one time. Max Yasgur's Aquarian Exposition turned into a monumental seething, writhing mass of cars, people, nudity, acid trips, in-the-mud-for-everyone-to-see sex, and a cloud of marijuana smoke over the whole thing that made it look like the L.A. basin during rush hour of a San Fernando Valley stage-three smog alert. That night Janet went on stage and put on the performance of a lifetime, but she managed to hit one sour note and stayed pissed about the whole thing for months.

In October she returned to Texas for a series of concerts that included Houston and Austin. Friends and family who attended could tell she needed help, but her father simply shook his head and told everyone that it was too late. Her show moved on to Tampa, Florida, where she got into a shouting match with police, who arrested her for using vulgar language in public when they tried to force her audience back into their seats. The charges were eventually dropped, but by that point she was a bigger junkie than Sinatra's *Man with the Golden Arm* ever thought about being, and her habit had advanced to the point that it required her to shoot all the way up to a handshaking acquaintance with that black-robed, bony-fingered dude carrying the scythe. She called it "shooting to death's door." By that point her career was on a full-tilt downhill slide fueled by booze, drugs, bisexual and tri-sexual liaisons, endless work, and the growing realization that being famous doesn't necessarily bring anything in the way of self-satisfaction or inner peace. If all this has begun to sound like a no-brakes bobsled ride straight into oblivion, that's exactly what it was.

The dawn of 1970 finally brought Janis to the realization that she had spent the previous ten years using everything from marijuana to heroin and that she needed to kick her habit. To that end she tried to remove herself from the company of her old doper buddies and did virtually everything she could to stay away from them and the temptations that could bring her back down.

In an obvious attempt to renew the feelings of family she had with Big Brother and the Holding Company, she dissolved the Kozmic Blues and formed a new group called the Full Tilt Boogie Band. Indications are that the creative powers honed on travel and experience over the years all came together with the Full Tilt boys. She hired vocal coaches, took voice lessons, and rededicated herself to the emotion and fun of her music. In addition she created the on-stage persona "Pearl" in an effort to separate her private self from the hard-driving, hard-drinking wild child her fans expected to see when she sang.

Janis and her new band performed along the East Coast for a bit, then traveled with some of her old friends on a train tour and rolling party that she said she would have done for no charge just to be there for the good times. She continued to stay away from drugs, but her consumption of Southern Comfort skyrocketed and had just as pernicious a set of consequences as the dope. In fact the liquor proved worse because it had a profoundly detrimental effect on her voice.

When the tour finished up and most of her band members fled to the tropics to relax, dangle their toes in the ocean, and soak up some

*Taken from original poster "The Other Side"* Created by Kevin Peake, 1988

sunshine, Janis flew back to Austin and attended the seventieth birthday party thrown for her close friend and mentor Kenneth Threadgill. From there she flew to San Diego and did one last gig with her old friends Big Brother and the Holding Company. The wild woman still came out when Janis performed, but the image took its toll on her, and it became increasingly difficult to maintain the separation she so desperately wanted. Friends have noted that she spoke of "Pearl" as though that portion of her personality and image could be kept in a box and put on like her feather boa and silk pants just before time to go on stage. It seemed to some that Janis Joplin had grown decidedly tired of being Janis Joplin.

By August 1970 she seemed completely willing and eager to confront the demons of her past and readied herself for the reunion of her graduating class back in Port Arthur. A few days prior to the big event, she appeared on Dick Cavett's late-night talk show again and admitted that the wounds inflicted during that period still hadn't scarred over and let everyone know of her intent to rub the noses of her former classmates in the money and power of her success. Her revenge didn't appear to take on any malevolent air, it seemed more like a big but nervous hoot for her. At any rate, things didn't work out the way she expected, and when the only recognition she received from the provincials was a little trophy for traveling the farthest to get back home for the night's festivities, she left town disappointed and downhearted by the lack of respect she had expected from the single group of people she needed it from more than any other.

Upon her arrival back in California, she met someone and fell head over whiskey bottle in love and started talking about having kids and spending the rest of her life in a nice little house with a picket fence, dogs, cats, and all the middle-class things she had spent the previous ten years running from. But she also openly worried about the effect her liquor consumption was having on her voice, cut back on the drinking, and started dabbling with heroin again.

In September the death of Jimi Hendrix got her undivided attention for at least a few minutes, but even that tragic event never managed to persuade her that her own death could follow if she didn't get her freshly rampaging drug use back under control. Barely three weeks later, while in Los Angeles working on her last recording, she and the most recent love of her life had a fight. Alone and depressed, Janis went to her Landmark Hotel room after a day of hard work on the new album, *Pearl,* and sometime during the night of October 5 she shot up with an unusually high concentration of heroin, collapsed between her bed and the wall, and never woke up. Well-known coroner to the stars Thomas Noguchi noted that the dope found on the scene checked in at 40 percent pure at a time when most of the stuff sold on the streets only managed a 1 or 2 percent concentration. Her death certificate officially recognizes "Acute Heroin-Morphine Intoxication" as the cause of her demise. As soon as she opened the balloon on that batch of stuff, her fate was sealed.

Road manager and friend John Cooke discovered the lifeless body of Janis Joplin. Acquaintances and family were shocked by her death of course, but nobody who actually knew her could really say with any degree of conviction that they were surprised. In accordance with a newly written will, the body was cremated and her ashes scattered in the ocean north of San Francisco.

Time has been extremely kind to Janis. A growing number of music critics now often refer to her as the "the best white blues singer in American musical history" or "the greatest female singer in the history of rock and roll." In 1979 Bette Midler starred in a popular but loosely biographical film rendition of Janis's life named *The Rose*. Although highly creative with the historic elements of her time with us, the movie does manage to capture the driving, let-it-all-hang-out, down-to-the-wire power of her on-stage presence and contrasts it with the absolute shocking self-destructive behavior that led to her death at the still young age of twenty-seven. Her passing closely paralleled that of a number of other famous singers including her idol, Bessie Smith, who also died from the ravages of drug and alcohol abuse.

And, in death, the hometown folks finally managed to come through with the recognition they had always withheld. In 1988 a crowd of 5,000 teary-eyed Port Arthur folks dedicated a bust of Janis that now resides at the Gates Memorial Library where she once worked. Fittingly they sang "Me and Bobby McGee" and wept over the loss of a daughter they had more than once ridiculed and ostracized.

# CHAPTER 15

———— ◦•◦ ————

# A BAD GIRL GONE GOOD
## Karla Faye Tucker

As has been mentioned in past chapters, one of the more depressing aspects of modern twenty-first-century life is its lack of colorful characters. Those women (and men for that matter) who would today be so bold as to think themselves in the same league as the likes of Sally Skull, Sarah Bowman, or Sophia Aughinbaugh Coffee Butts Porter generally fall into the large and ever growing ranks of copycat big behavers who do little more than entertain, shock, or both. In that respect a case could possibly be made for comparisons of such people to Adah Isaacs Menken, Belle Starr, or Bonnie Parker. No doubt our modern equivalents would all be found sorely lacking in the areas of originality and real individualism.

Sadly, instant renown for many today involves little more than a depressing life, topped off by deplorable acts of violence, and the televised end to the whole sad, unseemly mess. All of this is usually followed in short order by a horror-story-of-the-week-type book, a made for television movie, and instant notoriety for all those left behind in the wake of fleeting fame or wretched excess.

The short, sad biography of Karla Faye Tucker reads like a TV talk show producer's favorite daydream of just how bad it can be for a woman. As is the case with many such tales, and eerily like others in this book, little Karla started life in the most average and mundane manner. Born to middle-class parents in Houston, Texas, on November 18, 1959, she was the youngest in a family of three sisters whose names all cutely and oh-so-very-sixtyish-ly started with the same first letter. The oldest, Kathi Lynne, had two years on Karla, and the middle girl, Kari Ann, about a year.

As the family's "baby," Karla loved her dog, a German shepherd named Lady Bug, and other than a couple of instances of trying to set herself on fire and burn the house down while playing with matches, she led the kind of early life you would expect of most little girls. However, one of her passing flirtations with fire did result in third-degree burns to her left leg and a painful trip to a hospital emergency room where charred skin had to be scraped away, leaving scars which lasted a lifetime.

In numerous interviews this sad young woman always mentioned her father's vacation home on Caney Creek near Brazoria about forty-five miles southwest of Houston. Memories of the "bay house" seemed to be some of her favorite. During summer vacations she learned to pilot the family boat and took on the responsibility of seeing that it stayed gassed up so she and her sisters could spend their days pulling each other around the lake on skis.

Caney Creek also served as the site for her first efforts at learning to drive a car. Although so small she could barely see over the dash, the tiny eight-year-old loved careening along Brazoria's back roads where, as she liked to say, "there wasn't a whole lot you could hit."

But even at this early age she had reason to question and be suspicious of her own origins. Kathi Lynne and Kari Ann both enjoyed the attention straight blond hair, blue eyes, and fair-skinned beauty always attracts. Karla viewed her dark curly hair, bowed legs, olive complexion, and bony frame as ugly beyond her poor ability to describe. Acquaintances often wondered aloud if she had been adopted, and on more than one occasion Karla quizzed her parents along these same lines. They denied it, of course, and tried to reassure their daughter that nothing could be farther from the truth.

But their comforting words did little to stay the brutal assessment of childhood friends, and kids being kids, they made unmerciful fun of her because of her gnome-like appearance. They talked behind her back loud enough for Karla to hear and forced the insecure child into deeper and deeper feelings of rejection and isolation.

According to her own memory of the events, she took to smoking pot at some point between the ages of seven and eight. It all started when she caught her sisters puffing away on a number in the bathroom, and when confronted with that greatest of childhood threats, "I'll tell!" they quickly taught baby sister how to take a big toke on a doobie, and from then on little else in her life compared to the constancy of drugs. The most tired of all excuses gets used for this launching pad to oblivion: "All the kids were doing it."

The older girls' efforts did keep them from getting ratted out right then, but it really didn't matter. When Mama Carolyn actually caught Karla sucking on a joint a short time later, her response was to do exactly what any caring mom of the late sixties would. She brought out her own stash of dope and a packet of papers and forced the kid to roll one after another until she got it right. From then until the minute she stepped across a prison threshold, Karla Faye Tucker never knew a sober day. Fourteen years of hard-core drug use!

At about the age of ten, whatever might have remained of frilly dresses, playing with dolly, jumping rope, and roller skates vanished forever. Larry and Carolyn Tucker divorced. Tucker worked for years as a longshoreman on the Houston docks and for a time owned a portion of a company called Gulf Motorships. Karla has admitted that she never knew exactly why her parents parted, but given her mother's lifestyle afterward, it wouldn't be difficult to hazard a fairly accurate guess. It should be enough to note at this point that during a period when fathers seldom, if ever, got custody of their children during such proceedings, the court awarded Larry Tucker guardianship of all three of his daughters. This in spite of the fact that none of them wanted to go with him. According to Karla, Larry took his children out to a movie one night, and when they got home Mama Carolyn and everything she owned had simply disappeared from the scene.

The sisters were overcome with the emotional tragedy of it all, and shortly afterward Karla started on a whiz-bang downhill slide paved with sex, drugs, and rock and roll. At some point around the age of ten, after experimenting with marijuana for at least two years, a friend of sister Kari's offered the family's "baby" a ride on his motorbike and that all-time childhood favorite pastime "mainlining" heroin. She did a jack-knife and a half-twist off the high board, landed right in the middle of the sixties drug culture, and loved every minute of it.

Larry Tucker didn't know it and worked so much he didn't have time to do much of anything about it, but he had grabbed a three-tailed tiger and it was about to eat him alive. The man didn't smoke, drink, or swear and worked like a field hand to give his rebellious daughters absolutely anything they wanted. Unfortunately for him, the thing they wanted most was to live with their mother. Very simply put, poor ol' Larry spoiled his daughters rotten and they hated him for it. Discipline of any kind turned out to be futile, and hardly a day passed that Karla and the other girls didn't leave home, wait until their father went to work, and return to spend all their time doing drugs and damn near anything else they thought they were big enough to try.

In the beginning the older girls tended to be a bigger and more unmanageable problem than Karla. They would sneak out their bedroom windows, stay gone for extended periods, and come home so screwed up it would take two or three days just to get straightened out. In pretty short order Larry Tucker realized that he had absolutely no ability to control Kathi and Kari and gave in to their requests to go live with their mother.

Left alone with her father for about two years, Karla did everything she could to fulfill Larry Tucker's wish for a son. The tomboy in her loved playing football with him, and he often took her out for meals. She has described that interlude with her father as "a lot of fun." But by this point she had also become a full-fledged needle freak who never met a drug she didn't like. She loved the feel of the spike when it entered her flesh as much as the drug it supplied and consumed pills like they were popcorn. Placydil, Dilaudid, Soma, LSD, you name it she threw it down by the handful and absolutely couldn't get enough. Anyone trying to justify such behavior by using the old "escape from reality" excuse gets shot down by Karla's own words. She was a dopehead because of the way the drugs made her feel. End of story, period, paragraph, get on with it.

Eventually Larry Tucker had to give up and admit that when it came to his former wife and daughters, he was in so far over his head he couldn't see daylight. Karla went the way of her sisters. Fistfights at school, habitual truancy, lack of control, drug use, new problems by the minute, and when Daddy finally gave up, she landed smack dab in the middle of all the excitement of even greater drugs, real honest-to-god bad men, and Mama Carolyn.

Larry Tucker's innate decency might have been the thing that caused his eventual withdrawing from any relationship with his daughters. He just couldn't compete with the dark and visceral side of life his former wife had to offer. As far as she and the girls were concerned, "decent" translated as "square," and nobody in their right mind wanted to be "square" during those hip and groovy sixties and seventies. Anyway, Karla moved in with her mother, and that's when the adult fun and games really started.

Carolyn Moore Tucker lived what can only be described as a marginal lifestyle. Gnawing somewhere on her insides was a fatal attraction to men who lived on the fringes of the law and an unmanageable urge for all things unconventional including an insistence on never being judged by anything approaching societal norms. By day she worked a job at the Houston Police Department. When night came she did dope and turned tricks. Very simply put, Karla's Mama Carolyn was a high-dollar hooker who did her business over a red telephone that no one else in the house was allowed to answer. Carolyn was a hell of an example for a young girl to grow up with.

By the time she moved in with her mother and sisters, Karla had already tried sex. She remembered it as having happened at about the age of twelve or thirteen and freely admitted that the experience turned her into a "little sex fiend" on top of her status as a "little dope fiend." With baby daughter Karla's arrival, Mama Carolyn's four-bedroom apartment overflowed with seven women that included Carolyn, her four daughters, her best friend, and her daughter's best friend. All the girls in the house who looked old enough danced in "gentlemen's" clubs around Houston. Karla Faye never got a chance to take part in this particular bit of teenage fun and frolic because she just couldn't pull the age thing off. Didn't stop her from taking part though. She liked to hang around the clubs with her sisters and friends for the drinking and drugs that often follow such nighttime festivities. No one did anything to stop her.

Mama Carolyn's female doo-dah show and parade lived in the apartment for about a year before she remarried. Karla noted that the union was to an old man for his money and didn't last long. By then the self-destructive Carolyn had followed her daughters into hard drug use, and her life had started on an ever-spiraling downward run straight to oblivion.

At some point during this maelstrom of dope-induced looniness, Carolyn tried to introduce Karla to her biological father—her *real* father. Turns out Mama Carolyn had been messing around on Larry Tucker as early as two years after they married. And this particular messee was a Houston fireman of strong Greek descent, thus explaining Karla's unusual physical appearance. When confronted with the living, breathing realization that childhood friends who had wondered aloud about the possibility of adoption weren't far from wrong, Karla stared directly into the eyes of a man who looked exactly like her and said, "I already have a father." After a moment's hesitation to let her assessment sink in, she stomped out of the house, and indications are that Mama Carolyn never broached the subject again.

At the age of fifteen, when most girls should begin to actually take serious notice of boys for the first time and think in terms of coming graduations and prom dates, Karla Faye Tucker was an experienced prostitute, rock-and-roll groupie to some of the biggest names in the shake, jive, and jiggle biz back then, hard-core drug addict, and worst of all she didn't think there was even one little thing abnormal about her circumstances. The only small kink in her situation revolved around female problems that included painful menstrual flow and cysts on her ovaries. Her medical condition eventually resulted in a D & C at the age of thirteen and a hysterectomy two years later. An operation that most young women would have found devastating in the extreme simply meant no more worries about getting pregnant to a wild child of Karla's wacky worldliness and sexual adventurism.

At about the age of sixteen or seventeen—hey, it was the late seventies and definite dates and times didn't seem to take hold in a lot of folks' drug-addled brains when flowers were a-bloomin' and dope was free—Karla met and married what she deemed a hunky dreamboat of a carpenter named Steve Griffith. Not much else about her life changed with the marriage. As far as Karla and her tribe of traveling companions were concerned, men in such situations were expected to stay out of the way of an independent woman's "operating." But Griffith was possessive in the extreme, and they fought like cats and dogs the whole time they were together because of it. He even tried the old let's-live-with-my-mother routine, but the poor goober never had a chance with a hell on wheels woman like Karla. Their hasty and ill-advised marriage lasted about three years and ended with the death of Mama Carolyn.

On Christmas Eve 1979, at the still young age of forty-three, Carolyn Moore Tucker's life of living on the edge came to an early and abrupt halt. Years of drug abuse had resulted in a lengthy, losing battle with hepatitis. The disease ravaged a once beautiful woman, stole her life, and left a broken, empty shell behind. The only stabilizing influence in Karla's life was gone—such as it was. With Carolyn's passing, the cyclonic vortex of motel and convention "operating," rock band groupieism, biker babe belligerence, and folks who claimed to have been Green Beret assassins that made up her day-by-day existence pulled her inevitably to a rendezvous with the one man she'd have been better off having never met.

In 1981, while living in an apartment with her best friend and roommate at the time, a girl named Shawn Jackson, Karla made a trip to Midland for a week of "operating." She got back to Houston worn to a frazzle and found a Harley Davidson motorcycle sitting in the middle of her living room floor. The rug under it was saturated with black, greasy crankcase oil. Karla hit the roof like a roman candle ball. Any biker babe worth her salt understood that men always kept their Harleys in the living room, but something about this one just got all over her. She stormed up the stairs of their apartment and found Jerry Lynn Dean in her— Karla's—bed with best buddy Shawn. That fiery little gal jumped right in the middle of Dean with both feet and physically kicked him out of the apartment.

If she believed that was the end of Jerry Lynn Dean, she might have just as well taken a seat in her own coyote trap. A short time later the same scene got played out again, but in that instance she applied considerably more force. After seeing her boyfriend kicked out the second time and slapped silly on top of it, good buddy Shawn packed up and moved out. She eventually married Jerry Lynn Dean in spite of Karla's feelings about the man.

About two years after Shawn set up housekeeping with her number one love lump, she accompanied Karla on one of their little road trips. A sex, drugs, and rock-and-roll raid on New Orleans with a well-known band just proved too good to pass up for the girls. A furious Jerry Lynn Dean felt that Karla had talked his wife into "partying" with the group. In a fit of rage he rummaged around in his wife's belongings and found some photo albums of Karla's. He whipped out his knife and stabbed up a bunch of them and worst of all put holes in a picture of Mama Carolyn. Karla found out about the murder of her mother's sacred picture, and when Shawn came by with Dean the next day to pick up some clothing she'd left behind, the little spitfire ran out to the car and punched him in the eye so fast he didn't even have time to react. She broke Dean's spectacles in the process, and good buddy Shawn had to rush him to the emergency room and have slivers of glass removed from his eye. Karla's hatred for the man set up like concrete, and the feelings she had for him only got worse. It was the kind of hatred people like her end up living to regret.

That was in March of 1983, and by then Karla shared her tumultuous life with the man of her dreams. Pill-popping dopers like little Miss Tucker and her friends always knew where to find a Doctor Feel Good who would write a prescription for whatever they wanted. She met Danny Garrett while sitting in the waiting room of a local physician who supplied her with vast quantities of anything necessary to keep her high. Karla loved tough, hard-edged guys who knew how to handle themselves and the difficult situations they might get caught up in. Any man who carried a snub-nosed .38 in one boot and a bag of dope in the other was just the kind of bad-assed dude she couldn't resist. Danny Garrett reciprocated in kind and fell head over pistol-filled cowboy boots in love with the scrappy little tigress. The joyous lovers didn't waste a minute trying to maintain separate living arrangements and moved into a house at 2205 McKean in northwest Houston. Karla and Danny took one bedroom in the tiny residence and her sister Kari Tucker Burrell slept in another. Things worked like that with these people. Sometimes Kari and whoever she kept company with at the moment lived with Karla. Given a change in circumstances it might easily be the other way around. And of course every change of bed partners brought in a new batch of fringe people who just added to the sideshow atmosphere typical of such living arrangements. They came for a visit, slept over for days at a time, had sex in groups, and seldom ever attended Sunday school together.

Jimmy Leibrant fit into that fringe people category. He started hanging out at the house on McKean when Kari invited her ex-husband, Ronnie, to move in with Karla's new clan. Leibrant and Burrell had partnered up in the business of making speed for mass consumption. Added to this seething cauldron of tough guys, tougher gals, alcohol, drugs, prostitution, hatred for Jerry Lynn Dean, and guns, Ronnie Burrell was a singularly menacing figure in the mixture. Rumor had it that he would do whatever it took, to anybody, anytime, for any reason. Danny Garrett's brother Doug even went so far as to say he thought Ronnie was the devil, and there's every indication that he meant it.

All this craziness came to a bloody head in midsummer of 1983. For several days prior to June.13, Karla, her live-in companion Danny, and their "friend" Jimmy Leibrant spent every waking moment at the house on McKean shoveling anything even remotely like a drug into their mouths and arms. They drank, ingested everything from marijuana to pills of all varieties, shot speed and anything else they could get hold of. Such unfettered consumption of mind-altering chemicals can tend to have strange effects on the human psyche and body. At some point Leibrant got a case of the laying-around-doing-dope heebie-jeebies and started saying things like, "Oh god I've just gotta do something or I'm gonna go nuts."

When Garrett had finally heard it so many times his brains were about to leak out his ears, he grabbed paper and pencil and said, "Here's what we can do." He drew a floor plan for Jerry Lynn Dean's apartment. Karla had chanced upon the front door key to the place in some clothing of Shawn's she'd washed for her friend, and the plot quickly jelled as they left the house and headed for Dean's place. The initial thrust of their invasion was just to "case the joint." At various times they'd discussed stealing motorcycle parts from Dean for their own use—or for sale—and Karla had often talked of taking Dean's Harley away from him. In her estimation, any man who couldn't keep a tiny little girl like her from hitting him in the eye didn't deserve to have a bike like that. No one mentioned doing any real harm to Dean, but on the way out the door Garrett grabbed his shotgun. From that point on the lives of five people were strapped in for a roller-coaster ride straight downhill to a bad end.

Dean lived in a first-floor apartment on Watonga Street in the Oak Forest section of Houston. The three hyped-up, tighter-than-a-banjo-string, would-be commandos drove five and a half miles to get there, and Garrett parked his Chevy Ranchero near Dean's back door in the middle of a night barely lit by the snipped fingernail of a moon. Karla and Danny made their way from the rear of the apartment to the front door while Leibrant "scouted" to scope out what lights were on in which apartments and if anyone might be moving around outside. Karla would claim later that they still had no formal "plan" at this point. But they'd drawn pictures of the apartment, driven over five miles to get there, brought a shotgun, carried gloves, grabbed a hammer just in case, and then used unauthorized keys to break into another man's home. Such actions might seem like they were pretty well organized to even the most casual of observers. She even admitted that from the moment she shoved the key into the lock of Jerry's front door, the people inside didn't have a chance.

And so it all fell out that at approximately 3 a.m. on June 13, 1983, without realizing it, Karla Faye Tucker stood on the concrete front slab of number 2313 at Windtree Apartments and opened the tragic door to her own future. Danny Garrett swept past her and rushed toward the back bedroom where he knew Jerry Lynn Dean would be sleeping. Karla stayed right on his heels and later testified that shortly after Danny slipped into the dark hallway outside the sleeping man's bedroom, she heard Dean call out "What's going on?" Anyone who has ever been startled awake in the middle of the night by something they couldn't readily identify should understand how the man must have felt.

Karla pushed past Garrett, jumped on top of Dean, and told him to shut up. He had snapped bolt upright in a bed that was nothing more than a mattress on the floor. Dean must have recognized the person sitting straddle of him because he called her by name and did what he could to smooth out some of their past friction by saying something to the effect that, "We can work it out." Karla told him that if he moved or said another word he was a dead man.

When it comes to murder and craziness, there's always a point when things get weird, and here is where things in Jerry Lynn Dean's apartment got pretty strange. Anytime people are fighting for their lives in the dark, it can turn messy real fast, and that's exactly what happened.

Karla told this story several times, and it never changed. Hers is the only version available. After some tussling around, Dean evidently tired of having her on top of him and grabbed her by the arms just above the elbows. They wrestled around for a few more seconds before Danny Garrett pushed her aside and started hitting Jerry in the head with a heavy-duty ball-peen hammer Karla said he'd brought with him from his truck. The Houston Police Department never found the weapon she described. She claimed to have disposed of it after the killings. During the beating she jumped to her feet and turned the light on to get a better look at Danny's murderous skill level. Given that she could now see everything he did, it's pretty safe to assume that Karla Faye could recognize what he used to knock holes in ol' Jerry's noggin that night in spite of her level of drug intoxication. The medical examiner noted that tools of every description were scattered all over the bedroom and rather than a hammer, Danny might have used the blunt end of a pickax or even the butt of his shotgun. But Karla remained adamant about this particular fact and maintained from the beginning that the first blows came very specifically from a ball-peen hammer wielded by Danny Garrett. Hammer or not Danny went at it for so long and with such devotion to the enterprise that he worked up quite a sweat from his efforts. He finally got tired of swinging whatever he used on poor ol' Jerry and left Karla in the room with the dying man while he went out in the hall for a breather.

Dean had somehow managed to fall over facedown. Garrett had struck his victim so forcefully on top of the head that the man's skull had detached from his spinal column. When the human cranium is no longer attached to the neck in such a fashion, breathing passages begin to fill with blood and other fluids. This unnatural movement of liquids in the body causes loud, unsettling, almost inhuman bubbling and gurgling sounds.

A small cut on the scalp usually results in an amazing amount of blood flow. Having a grown man whack someone on the head with a hammer or other blunt instrument till he got tired would create a tableau of such horror most people would leave the gory scene so fast their running shoes would probably lay down scorch marks on the carpet. Not Karla Faye Tucker. She stayed with Jerry's oozing corpse and became obsessed with the gurgling noises coming from it. " I kept hearing that sound and all I wanted to do was stop it. I wanted to stop him from making that noise. . . ."

She glanced quickly around the cluttered bedroom and spotted a three-foot-long pickax leaned against the wall. Dean worked for a cable television company and needed the tool to bury cables that ran from telephone poles to the houses he serviced. Digging a trench in Houston's rock-hard gumbo soil and thick St. Augustine grass required an instrument of such weight and authority. The user of that sod-busting implement needed strength and more than a little bit of gutsy determination.

By now Jimmy Leibrant had returned from his "scouting" mission and could hear the wheezing from Jerry's battered carcass all the way to the apartment's open front door. He later described the sound as similar to what you would expect a water pump sucking air to make. He strolled up to the bedroom and peeped inside just in time to see little Karla do a double overhanded swing and sink the pickax in Jerry Lynn Dean's back. Then he headed for the great outdoors like a scalded dog, hot-footed it back down to Watonga, found a pay phone, and called Ronnie Burrell to come pick him up. Stealing motorcycle parts was one thing, but brutal murder of the sort Leibrant had just witnessed was a com-pletely different animal altogether.

Karla continued whacking at Jerry with the pickax but couldn't make any headway toward stopping those pesky noises. They were driving her nuts. Danny, who'd been loading motorcycle parts into his truck, came back—probably because Karla couldn't get the job done—rolled Dean onto his back, and left the pickax sticking out of the seriously hacked up man's chest. He then stomped off again just about the time Karla real-ized that someone else was in the room, hidden under some bedcovers at the foot of the mattress next to the wall.

Her friend Shawn Jackson Dean had not lived with Jerry Lynn for some time. Karla must have reasoned that whoever whimpered under those sheets wasn't her longtime running buddy. In fact the woman trying to hide from death that night was Deborah Ruth Thornton, a thirty-two-year-old bookkeeper Dean had befriended at a pool party the previous afternoon. Karla grabbed the pickax again and took a swing at the quaking person she couldn't even see. Her rushed lick barely grazed the intended victim and forced her make a second attempt. At that point Deborah Thornton sat up, grabbed the pickax, and fought like a tiger to stop the assault. In the middle of the life-and-death struggle between the two women for control of the murder weapon, Danny Garrett popped back onto the scene, pulled them apart, shoved Karla aside, and went back to work with the gruesome weapon.

Karla stumbled out of the room for a bit and returned later to find Deborah Thornton in a sitting position with the pickax's blade buried up to the handle in her left shoulder. Danny loomed over the wounded woman who cried, "Oh, God, it hurts. If you are going to kill me, please hurry up." Garrett promptly kicked her in the head and jerked the pickax loose in one quick set of muscular movements. Deborah Ruth Thornton fell onto her back just in time to receive a killing blow that punched through her heart and left the cutting edge of the heavy digging tool seven inches deep in her chest.

When most people consider the scene just described, they think that the first thing they would do—if they were the murderers, of course—is skip town faster'n you could blow out a candle. Did Karla and Danny run for the wilds of Idaho, Montana, Mexico, or Canada? Did they go into hiding at another location in Houston? Did they stay zip-lipped about the horrific killings and how they felt about them? Not a chance, good buddies, not a chance. They went right back to the McKean Street house, carried on with their dope-addled lives as though it didn't mean a thing, and even bragged to friends and family about their involvement in the murders.

That loose-mouthed attitude frightened the hell out of Danny's brother Doug and Karla's sister Kari. Kari had moved out of the house by that time. A little over a month after the crime, Doug Garrett called the Houston Police Department and told homicide detective J. C. Mosier that his brother Danny and Danny's girlfriend Karla Faye Tucker were responsible for what Houston newspapers referred to as "The Pickax Murders." Mosier, a former Oak Forest boy, couldn't believe his ears. He knew Garrett in a kind of backhanded way—an old friend from high school had been married to Danny at some point.

But what it all came down to was that Karla and Danny's bragging and nonstop talk of the killings kept getting blacker and more frightening with every minute that passed. What they had done went way beyond reason or sanity, but that wasn't the worst of it. All the wind-bellied, flannel-mouthed talk had now swung around to the possibility that they might even have to get rid of some other people just to protect themselves. Jimmy Leibrant and Ronnie Burrell headed a list of prospective victims that couldn't do anything but get longer with every passing day.

And more damning than all that, according to both Doug and Kari, Karla had openly claimed she experienced a rush of sexual satisfaction every time she hit Jerry Lynn Dean with the pickax. The confession proved too much for Doug and Kari to take. In fact that single revelation probably did more to seal Karla's fate than any other piece of evidence later presented at her trial.

Homicide detectives had already questioned everyone from the McKean house. Since they all knew Jerry Lynn Dean and were aware of Karla's antagonism toward him, it was only natural that the portion of the investigation that centered on Dean's murder included them. Doug and Kari went into something like a state of walking shock after having viewed crime scene photographs that ended with a particularly ghastly picture of Deborah Thornton on her back with the pickax sticking out of her chest. At its absolute bottom line Doug and Kari were accessories after the fact for their knowledge of the crime and their efforts to help protect their relatives by hiding and destroying evidence. It didn't take long for the whole bubbling brain mangler presented to them by police to have a profound effect.

After a night of terrified introspection, Doug Garrett and Kari Tucker Burrell decided to tell it all. But Detective Mosier was a careful man. He wanted the story of the murders to come directly from the mouths of those responsible for the killings. He arranged for representatives of the Special Crimes Bureau to fit Doug with a miniature transmitter-tape recorder and taught the terrified man how to get the killers to engage in the kind of chitchat that would lead to confessions of their intent to take the life of and steal from Jerry Lynn Dean along with Karla's bizarre tale of sexual gratification.

At about 5:00 p.m. on July 20, 1983, Doug Garrett rode his motorcycle up to the house on McKean, walked inside, and started the bullshit ball rolling with his brother and Karla Faye Tucker. He left at a little after 6:00 carrying a tape recording of everything law enforcement could possibly have hoped for. By 7:00 police had arrested Jimmy Leibrant—who appeared out of nowhere after several days' absence—Danny, and Karla. From that instant till the day they died, Karla and Danny never saw another moment of freedom.

On April 23, 1984, after a trial that lasted just under two weeks, a jury of eight women and four men found Karla Faye Tucker guilty of capital murder. In Texas there are two distinct parts for any trial that might involve the eventual execution of the defendant. There's the guilt or innocence phase followed by a punishment phase. During the punishment phase the jury must decide two separate questions: whether the conduct that caused the death of the victim was committed deliberately and with reasonable expectation that death would result, and whether there is a probability that the defendant will commit criminal acts of violence that will constitute a continuing threat to society. A yes vote on both questions insures the death penalty. No on either question or both, and the defendant goes to prison for life.

In an effort to put a human face on Karla Faye Tucker, her lawyers let her tell her own story for the jury. Some considered that move a serious error in judgment. What came out was simply a more detailed version of the account you've just read. It didn't take those eight women and four men but three hours to decide "yes" on both the questions before them. Afterwards jurors willing to talk about the case said they didn't want to lay a death penalty on Karla, but just couldn't find any way out of it.

In December 1984, after Danny Garrett's trial also ended in a guilty verdict based primarily on Karla's testimony, she was moved to the Mountain View unit of the Texas State Department of Corrections across State Highway 36 from Gatesville. She had just celebrated her twenty-fifth birthday.

That probably should have been the end of Karla Faye Tucker's story. No woman had been legally executed in Texas since Chipita Rodriguez, and deep down pretty much everyone involved in her case must have felt that the chances Karla would be the first since the Civil War were virtually nonexistent. Some participants in the trial have claimed they believed all along that her execution was inevitable. Maybe, maybe not. All the social indicators of the early 1980s pointed to a long and uneventful life in prison that would most likely end with her death as the result of old age.

But from her first moment in custody at the Harris County lockup, the infamous "Pickax Murderess" began to change in ways no one who had ever known her could possibly have predicted. Cut off from her always-there-in-the-past clan of tough-talking, borderline criminal men, no way to "operate," no drugs, and no sisters or other women to impress with her hard-as-nails persona, something had to give.

The remarkable transformation started slowly as she fumbled her way past the muddy curtain of drug-induced intoxification that had been a minute-by-minute way of life for almost fifteen years. In December 1983, four months after her arrest and following close on the heels of her twenty-fourth birthday, she attended her first Alcoholics Anonymous meetings and Bible study classes. More importantly, she met Chaplain Rebecca Lewis, who turned out to be one of the most influential people Karla ever knew. Lewis listened, counseled, advised, and eventually allowed Karla to join her advanced Bible classes. These study groups were strictly reserved for those inmates Lewis believed sincere in their conversions—not just "playing church." She expected the hand-picked women allowed to take part in the group to perform a missionary-style role when they returned to the tank and conduct their own classes for fellow inmates. Karla Faye Tucker proved to be her best-known success story.

From that point until early 1998, even the harshest of dyed-in-the-wool conservatives involved in her case have admitted their belief in the sincerity of Karla's Christian redemption and freely noted her relentless efforts to help others who might have followed in her footsteps. Unfortunately a change of character and good works did little to stop the relentless tide of failed appeals.

During the last few months of her life, she once again became a celebrity of sorts—a notorious person of even greater import than any she ever garnered when on trial in Houston fourteen years earlier. She cheerfully agreed to a number of televised interviews—the most notable being one with Larry King on January 14, 1998—and managed to single-handedly focus the harsh spotlight of national and international media scrutiny on the issue of capital punishment.

But in the end nothing else about her life before or after the murders mattered in the minds of most people except her appointment with destiny on Tuesday, February 3, 1998. That evening at approximately 6:30 p.m. CST her five personally selected witnesses and at least one member of the press were ushered into the viewing area of the Huntsville death chamber.

Karla lay strapped to a gurney on the opposite side of a double set of plastic windows. She wore typical prison issue white shirt, pants, and white running shoes. Once the witnesses settled down, Warren Morris Jones, who stood near Karla inside the death chamber, asked if she had any final words.

She turned her head slightly and directed her first comments to attending survivors of Deborah Ruth Thornton. "Yes sir. I would like to say to all of you—the Thornton family and Jerry Dean's family—that I am so sorry. I

*Photo from Karla Faye's Home Page on LifeWay Services website* Photo by Ron Kuntz/Reuters

hope God will give you peace with this." She said goodbye to her husband, Dana Brown, a man she had married while in prison and finished with, "I love all of you very much. I am going to be face to face with Jesus now. Warden Baggett, thank all of you so much. You have been so good to me. I love all of you very much. I will see you all when you get there. I will wait for you." She closed her eyes and said a silent prayer. The chemical brew necessary for lethal injection flowed through the plastic tubing leading to the needles in both arms, and four minutes later Huntsville doctor Daryl Wells entered the chamber, checked each eye with a tiny flashlight, held a finger to her neck for a pulse, repeated the process with a stethoscope, and announced, "6:45." The warden repeated, "6:45" and the short, sad, tragic life of a bad girl gone good ended.

Worldwide attention vanished like cold water thrown on a depot stove in January as soon as word of her death hit the news media's satellite dishes. Three days later a few family members and friends stood by her grave at Forest Park Lawndale Cemetery in Houston and said a final goodbye as Karla Faye Tucker was buried.

—◆—

Almost exactly a year after what might well go down in history as Texas's most famous execution, a sixty-two-year-old gray-haired, frumpy-looking great-grandmother and former death-row friend of Karla Faye's named Betty Lou Beets took her place in the pantheon of female criminals as the second woman to be legally executed in Texas since the Civil War. Newspaper reports didn't even bother to include poor ol' Chipita's name that time around—a graphic indication of how quickly the rabble doth forget.

The state of Texas sent Ms. Beets on her fatal journey because she shot her fifth husband Jimmy Don in the back of the head and buried him under a fake wishing well in the front yard of their doublewide trailer house in Gun Barrel City. Authorities indicted but never brought her to trial for the killing of her fourth husband, Doyle Wayne Barker, whose body somehow managed to get its shot-in-the-head self under a shed not far from her infamous husband under the wishing well. Hubby number three totally and completely vanished like a puff of smoke and has never been heard from or seen since. And at some point she even managed to plead guilty to a charge of shooting her second husband and attempting to run him over with a pickup truck. Lucky devil somehow managed to get away alive.

In the waning months of 1999, after almost a decade and a half in prison, the absolute reality of her imminent demise settled in and Ms. Beets, affectionately called the "Black Widow" by the news media, started giving interviews right and left. She claimed—in the best politically correct fashion—to have been physically and psychologically abused by all of her husbands including the two buried in her front yard and any others she might or might not have been forced to bust a cap on. When that didn't work, she tried to blame it all on her son. Death penalty opponents of every stripe came out of the woodwork to endorse her belated assertions, but the state of Texas wasn't buying any of it. Nor did hardly anyone else.

While Betty's appointment with her Maker did draw a small crowd, it couldn't come anywhere close to the emotional outpouring that surrounded Ms. Tucker's exit. A protest gathering of fewer than a hundred and less than fifty media types just didn't compare with the more than 1,200 to 1,400 spectators and 200-plus talking heads from around the world who met the previous year to assist Karla on her journey into the next life.

The contrasts between the two women's lives and how they chose to meet death didn't stop there. Betty spent her last day with a few friends and relatives, refused a final meal, and requested that family members not attend the execution. She made no final statement and asked no forgiveness of any member of the victims' families, several of whom were in attendance. On Thursday, February 24, 2000, she lay strapped to the same table where Karla left this world, coughed twice, and was pronounced dead at 6:18 p.m.

The number of women who await the end of their lives on death row in Texas and around the nation is now greater in our country than ever before and continues to grow almost daily. No doubt another heartrending tale possessed of even more drama, passion, and rampant weirdness than that of Karla Faye Tucker will manifest itself at some point in the future. But given modern America's universal penchant for quickly forgetting the immediate moment's drain on our national tear duct, the probability exists that those women who follow Karla into death's open arms will never achieve her luminous and highly effecting moment in the glaring limelight of popular culture.

# BIBLIOGRAPHY

———•●•———

## Books

Abernethy, Francis Edward. *Legendary Ladies of Texas: Publications of the Texas Folklore Society Number XLIII* (Dallas: E-Heart Press, 1981).

Burton, Art. *Black, Red, and Deadly* (Austin: Eakin Publications, Inc., 1991).

Cannon, Bill. *A Treasury of Texas Trivia* (Plano, Texas: Republic of Texas Press, 1997).

Chariton, Wallace O. *This Dog'll Hunt—An Entertaining Texas Dictionary* (Plano, Texas: Wordware Publishing, 1989–1990).

Cunningham, Eugene. *Triggernometry* (New York: Barnes & Noble Books, 1996).

Drago, Gail. *Etta Place—Her Life and Times with Butch Cassidy and The Sundance Kid* (Plano, Texas: Republic of Texas Press, 1996).

Drago, Gail, and Ann Ruff. *Outlaws in Petticoats* (Plano, Texas: Republic of Texas Press, 1995).

Friedman, Myra. *Buried Alive: The Biography of Janis Joplin.* (New York: Harmony, 1992)

Froebel, Julius. *Seven Years Travel in Central America, Northern Mexico, and the Far West of the United States* (London, United Kingdom: Richard Bentley, 1859).

Harman, S. W. *Hell on the Border* (Lincoln: University of Nebraska Press-Bison Books, 1992).

Hutson, Jan. *The Chicken Ranch—The True Story of the Best Little Whorehouse in Texas* (Cranbury, New Jersey: A.S. Barnes and Co., Inc., 1980).

Jameson, W. C. *Bubba Speak—Texas Folk Sayings* (Plano, Texas: Republic of Texas Press, 1998).

———. *Unsolved Mysteries of the Old West* (Plano, Texas: Republic of Texas Press, 1999).

Jenkins, John H., and H. Gordon Frost. *I'm Frank Hamer—The Life of a Texas Peace Officer* (Austin: The Pemberton Press, 1968).

Keyes, Ralph. *Is There Life After High School?* (New York: Warner Books, 1976).

Knight, Oliver. *Fort Worth: Outpost On the Trinity* (Norman, Oklahoma: University of Oklahoma Press, 1953).

London, Marvin E. *Famous Court Trials of Montague County* (St. Jo, Texas: S.J.T. Printers, 1976).

Lowery, Beverly. *Crossed Over—A Murder, A Memoir* (New York: Alfred A. Knopf, 1992).

Metz, Leon C. *El Paso Chronicles—A Record of Historical Events in El Paso, Texas* (El Paso, Texas: Mangan Books, 1993).

———. *John Wesley Hardin—Dark Angel of Texas* (El Paso, Texas: Mangan Books, 1996).

———. *The Shooters* (El Paso, Texas: Mangan Books, 1976).

O'Neal, Bill. *Encyclopedia of Western Gunfighters* (Norman, Oklahoma: University of Oklahoma Press, 1979).

Rosa, Joseph, G. *The Gunfighter—Man or Myth?* (Norman, Oklahoma: University of Oklahoma Press, 1969).

Sandwich, Brian. *The Great Western: Legendary Lady of the Southwest* (El Paso, Texas: Texas Western Press, 1990).

Selcer, Richard E. *Hell's Half Acre—The Life and Legend of a Red-Light District* (Fort Worth: Texas Christian University Press, 1991).

Shirley, Glen. *Law West of Fort Smith* (Lincoln: University of Nebraska Press-Bison Books, 1968).

## Chapters and Parts of Books

Alexander, Stanley G. "Janis and the Austin Scene." In *Legendary Ladies of Texas,* edited by Francis E. Abernethy (Dallas: E-Heart Press, 1981).

Britton, Morris L. "Porter, Sophia Suttenfield." In *New Handbook of Texas* (Austin: The Texas State Historical Association, 1996).

Burton, Art. "Bass Reeves: The Invincible Marshal." In *Black, Red, and Deadly* (Austin: Eakin Press, 1991).

Cunningham, Eugene. "The Hammer Thumb." In *Triggernometry* (New York: Barnes & Noble Books, 1996).

Drago, Gail, and Ann Ruff. "Belle Starr-The Petticoat Terror." In *Outlaws in Petticoats* (Plano, Texas: Republic of Texas Press, 1995).

——. "Sally Skull-The Two Gun Terror." In *Outlaws in Petticoats* (Plano, Texas: Republic of Texas Press, 1995).

——. "Sarah Bourjett Bowman—The Great Western." In *Outlaws in Petticoats* (Plano, Texas: Republic of Texas Press, 1995).

——. "Sophia Suttenfield Aughinbaugh Coffee Butt Porter." In *Outlaws in Petticoats* (Plano, Texas: Republic of Texas Press, 1995).

Ellison, Samuel, Jr. "Barrow, Clyde Chesnut." *New Handbook of Texas* (Austin: Texas State Historical Association, 1996).

Frost, H. Gordon. "El Paso Madams." In *Legendary Ladies of Texas,* edited by Francis E. Abernethy. (Dallas: E-Heart Press, 1981).

Harman, S. W. "Belle Starr, The Female Desperado." In *Hell on the Border* (Lincoln: Bison Books, 1992).

Hughes, Richard B. "Joplin, Janis Lyn." In *New Handbook of Texas* (Austin: Texas State Historical Association, 1996).

Jenkins, John H. "Hamer, Francis Augustus." In *New Handbook of Texas* (Austin: Texas State Historical Association, 1996).

Kilgore, Dan. "Scull, Sarah Jane Newman." In *New Handbook of Texas* (Austin: Texas State Historical Association, 1996).

——."Two Six-Shooters and a Sunbonnet: The Story of Sally Skull." In *Legendary Ladies of Texas,* edited by Francis E. Abernethy (Dallas: E-Heart Press, 1981).

London, Marvin E "The Hanging of Nancy Hill." In *Famous Trials of Montague County* (St. Jo, Texas: S.J.T. Printers, 1976).

Long, Christopher. "Barrow, Clyde Chesnut." In *New Handbook of Texas* (Austin: Texas State Historical Association, 1996).

——. "Old Three Hundred." In *New Handbook of Texas* (Austin: Texas State Historical Association, 1996).

Maguire, Jack. "Sophia Porter—Texas' Own Scarlett O'Hara." In *Legendary Ladies of Texas* (Dallas: E-Heart Press, 1981).

McDonald, Archie P. "Runaway Scrape." In *New Handbook of Texas* (Austin: Texas State Historical Association, 1996).

McNeely, Regina Bennett. "Bowman, Sarah." In *New Handbook of Texas* (Austin: Texas State Historical Association, 1996).

Metz, Leon C. "Hardin, John Wesley." In *New Handbook of Texas* (Austin: Texas State Historical Association, 1996).

——. "Starr, Myra Maybelle Shirley." In *New Handbook of Texas* (Austin: Texas State Historical Association, 1996).

Phillips, John Neal, and Andre L. Gorzell. "Tell Them I Don't Smoke Cigars." In *Legendary Ladies of Texas,* edited by Francis E. Abernethy (Dallas: E-Heart Press, 1981).

Pilcher, Walter, E "Chicken Ranch." *New Handbook of Texas* (Austin: Texas State Historical Association, 1996).

Selcer, Richard E. "Hell's Half-Acre, Fort Worth." In *New Handbook of Texas* (Austin: Texas State Historical Association, 1996).

———. "Porter, Fannie." In *New Handbook of Texas* (Austin: Texas State Historical Association, 1996).

Shirley, Glen. "Lady Desperado." In *Law West of Fort Smith* (Lincoln: University of Nebraska Press-Bison Books, 1968).

Storey, John W. "Port Arthur, Texas." In *New Handbook of Texas* (Austin: Texas State Historical Association, 1996).

Strickland, Kristi. "Parker, Bonnie." In *New Handbook of Texas* (Austin: Texas State Historical Association, 1996).

Underwood, Marylynn. "The Ghost of Chipita: The Crying Woman of San Patricio." In *Legendary Ladies of Texas* (Dallas: E-Heart Press, 1981).

———."Rodriguez, Josefa." In *New Handbook of Texas* (Austin: Texas State Historical Association, 1996).

Wegenhoft, Victor C. "Rabb, William." In *New Handbook of Texas* (Austin: Texas State Historical Association, 1996).

Weingarten, Ruthe. "Belle Starr—The Bandit Queen of Dallas." In *Legendary Ladies of Texas* (Dallas: E-Heart Press, 1981).

Wheeler, Keith. "And now... showtime." In *The Townsmen—The Old West* (Alexandria, Virginia: Time-Life Books, Inc., 1975).

Young, Barbara L. "Newman, Joseph." In *New Handbook of Texas* (Austin: Texas State Historical Association, 1996).

## Newspaper and Magazine Articles-Memoirs

Associated Press. "First woman since Civil War faces Execution" (Dallas: *Dallas Morning News,* December 19, 1997)

———. "Karla Faye Tucker buried in quiet Houston ceremony" (Dallas: *Dallas Morning News,* February 7, 1998).

Beaty, Mrs. Cyle Gear. "Savage Days in Springtown" (Stillwater, Oklahoma: *Old West,* Winter 1966).

Biffle, Kent. "Texana—Women don't often meet the Executioner" (Dallas: *Dallas Morning News,* November 13, 1994).

Bingham, Larry. "The hanging of Chipita" (Fort Worth: *Fort Worth Star-Telegram,* January 7, 1998).

Bradfield, J. R. Jr. "Long Hunt Over Three States Is Ended As Six Officers Ambush Pair in Speeding Auto" (Dallas: *Dallas Morning News,* May 24, 1934).

Campbell, Robert C. "When Death Danced With Eleven" (Weatherford, Texas: *The Weatherford Democrat,* 1949).

Ford, John S. "Memoirs" (Austin: University of Texas Archives-IV, p. 645).

Horner, Kim. "A history of havoc—tour revisits stomping grounds of legendary Bonnie and Clyde" (Dallas: *Dallas Morning News,* April 23, 2000).

Hope, Christy. "Tucker put to death amid raging debate" (Dallas: *Dallas Morning News,* February 4, 1998).

Hunter, J. Marvin. "Heel-Fly Times In Texas: A Story of the Civil War Period" (Bandera, Texas: *Frontier Times,* 1924, page 38).

———. "Woman Hanging Called Incident" (Bandera, Texas: *Frontier Times,* March 1931, page 288).

Jennings, Dianne. "Beets executed for husband's murder" (Dallas: *Dallas Morning News,* February 23, 2000).

Jordan, Henderson. "Arcadia Sheriff Tells How Barrow Drove Into Trap" (Dallas: *Dallas Morning News*, May 24, 1934).

O'Conner, Colleen. "The Madam Mystique" (Dallas: *Dallas Morning News,* September 21, 1993).

Pederson, Rena. "The Betty Beets Legacy" (Dallas: *Dallas Morning News,* February 27, 2000).

Stovall, Waltrina. "Author formed bond with condemned Killer" (Dallas: *Dallas Morning News,* January 28, 1998).

Wicks, Jerome. "The Best Little Sequel on Broadway?" (Dallas: *Dallas Morning News,* May 8, 1994).

# INDEX

# ABOUT THE AUTHOR

J. Lee Butts' first novel debuted in November 2001 and has since been followed by numerous works. Magazine and short works include features for *True West*, *New American Review*, and Western Writers of America's *Roundup* magazine. Nonfiction works are *Texas Bad Girls* and *Texas Bad Boys*.